Dad's Guide to Twins

How to Survive the Twin Pregnancy and Prepare for Your Twins

Joe Rawlinson

dadsguidetotwins.com

Dad's Guide to Twins

Third Edition

Cover Design: Momir Borocki

ISBN 978-1482372274

Published by Texadero LLC, Austin, Texas

To my beautiful wife
and darling daughters

Why This Book?

Dads are forgotten in the world of pregnancy and parenthood books.

There are countless books on how to get ready for kids, most of which are written for moms, by moms. If we're lucky, we dads might get a shout-out.

Guidance for twins or multiples is nearly as sparse as help for dads. Even when you move to the specialty twin books for expectant parents, dads are mostly relegated to footnotes.

When my wife and I were expecting our twins, I couldn't find any great sources of information for dads expecting twins. I figure if I had that trouble, other fathers like you probably need information, too.

I wrote this book to help you learn from my experiences so you can be the best twin dad you can be.

About the Author

I'm Joe Rawlinson, the father of four children: two boys and identical twin girls. When our twins were born, our boys were 3 years old and 21 months old.

We proudly proclaimed that we had four kids ages 3 and under. That proclamation quickly gave way to the reality of caring for those four kids ages 3 and under. Needless to say, we had our hands full and still do!

I think twins are a blast and love mine to pieces. I just wish I knew what I know now before the whole twin adventure began. I've taken what I learned and have helped thousands of parents expecting twins through my blog, podcast, and books (this one you're reading and its sequel "Dad's Guide to Raising Twins: How to Thrive as a Father of Twins").

Disclaimer and Fine Print

The tips and insights offered in this book are based on my own experience and research. There may be inaccuracies, errors, and even a heavy dose of my own opinion.

I'm not a doctor. Be sure to consult your twins' pediatrician and your wife's OB/GYN doctor on all health matters. I'm not an accountant or lawyer either, so on financial and legal matters, double check with them, too.

Every twin pregnancy is different and your experience will be different from mine. In fact, I hope it will be better if you implement some of my tips and advice.

Contents

Chapter One

Emotional Roller Coaster

How We Found Out

My wife and I found out we were having twins on Christmas Eve. My wife had her first doctor visit of the pregnancy mid-morning. This was the routine visit that you set up as soon as you know you're pregnant.

With our two previous children, this visit was simply a confirmation of what the home pregnancy test already told us.

This day, however, would be different.

Because I was working under the assumption that this was just a normal doctor visit, I dropped my wife off at the doctor's office and drove our two boys around while we waited for her to be done.

As we sat in a store parking lot killing time, I got a call on my cell phone. It was my wife telling me that she was done.

I asked how things went and she said they went well and that she got an ultrasound. That was a big surprise to me since we'd never had an ultrasound so early with our previous pregnancies. Maybe, I thought, it was a little slow at the doctor's office that day.

I asked how the ultrasound went. She said they saw healthy heartbeats.

"That's great," was my reply before I stopped and asked, "Did you say heartbeats? Plural?"

Yes, we're having twins!

"OK, I'll be right there." I hung up and drove in a shell-shocked daze back to the doctor's office.

> FROM YOUR FELLOW FATHER OF TWINS...
> "We went to the doctor's office; my wife got set up for the ultrasound, and we were told, 'Oh, I see one, and right behind it we see number two. And we have two heartbeats.' We were completely floored. It felt like the oxygen got sucked from the room. It was so much of a surprise and just an unbelievable moment to find out that we were having twins." - Christos Xidias

Nine Things Every Dad Feels When He Learns He Is Having Twins

When you find out that you are having twins, you will experience a range of emotions. For me, my emotions ran the gamut for about six weeks. The news of twins can really rock your world!

You may have already experienced this array of feelings, too.

Fear

Fear of what? Fear of the unknown. You realize that having twins will not be easy. You're not afraid of hard work, but you don't know what your reality will be.

One solution: Fear not, my friend. Many have gone down this road before. We're here to help.

Poor

You find yourself thinking, "How am I going to afford twins?" Your mind races ahead to double everything – clothes, bikes, college tuition, weddings, etc.

One solution: Think "used." Used clothes, strollers, car seats, toys, etc., are all great to help ease the financial burden of twins in the early years. Unfortunately, you can't really get "used" college tuition, so use your hard-earned money to your advantage in the early years of twin life.

Cramped

You find yourself thinking, "How am I going to fit all these kids in my current house? Where will they sleep? Where will we put double the baby stuff, like strollers, car seats, baby swings, and the rest?"

One solution: Unless you're in a one-bedroom apartment, you don't necessarily have to go buy a new house to accommodate your twins. You can make do with what you have. More on that later.

Sick

You may have felt sick to your stomach as you tried to process all of these emotions and thoughts. You may have felt nervous with a mix of feeling overwhelmed and stressed. You also may not get much sleep that first night (or beyond) because your mind is racing as you try to process the news.

One solution: Don't eat much if you feel sick to your stomach. Stick with liquids so you don't get dehydrated. Resort to protein bars or shakes to keep your caloric intake up. Take a nap if you can, or go to bed early the next night.

Helpless

Odds are, these are your first twins. They may even be your first kids. The thought, "What am I supposed to do?" has likely crossed your mind.

One solution: Remember that there are plenty of other fathers of twins out there. If we can do it, so can you. Don't be afraid to ask us for help.

Skeptical

You find yourself thinking, "Really? My wife looks the same. Is she really pregnant with twins?" Your ultrasounds are surreal. Yes, there are two little heartbeats. But it is hard to believe it is real.

One solution: Pinch yourself. It is real. They don't fake ultrasounds except in the movies and on TV.

Logistically Challenged

"How can I possibly care for two babies at the same time?" Taking care of one baby seems overwhelming enough. "How can I physically hold, cuddle, change, dress, soothe, or feed two at once?"

One solution: Get helpers. If you are alone with the kids, it is fine to have your babies take turns. Change one at a time. Feed one at a time.

Nervous

You'll be nervous about holding and handling your tiny twin babies. They will be so small and seemingly fragile. You're probably thinking, "What if I hurt them?"

One solution: Before our first child was born, my wife and I took a class at the hospital that included things like how to hold a baby, how to change a diaper, and how to dress a baby, among other things. Look for a class like this in your area.

Another idea is to find friends who have babies and pay them a visit to practice holding an infant.

Take heart in the fact that babies are very resilient and flexible, and they won't break if you're gentle.

Excited

You're going to be a father of twins. You are in an elite fraternity. That is awesome! If you ever wanted to prove what a great dad you are, this is your chance.

One solution: Keep the excitement. Journal your feelings so you can recall the happy anticipation as you began this amazing journey. Look forward to playing with your twins, and don't be afraid to make plans for the fun times ahead.

Be Ready for Anything

Every twin pregnancy has its own unique challenges, and yours will be no different. I thought of the twin births of a few friends, and each ended distinctly:

- Near full term pregnancy with both twins delivered vaginally. The babies went home when mom did.
- Delivery at 33 weeks with an emergency C-section. The premature babies landed in the Neonatal Intensive Care Unit (NICU) for about a month.
- Delivery at 36 weeks with a scheduled C-section. The twins went home with mom and dad.
- Boys delivered at 38 weeks via emergency C-section. One ended up in the NICU for a week while one went home with Mom and Dad.
- Twins were delivered by emergency C-section at 32 weeks. The boys spent about six weeks in NICUs in two separate hospitals. One twin underwent abdominal surgery.

The moral of the story is that you should be ready for whatever comes. Even if you are planning on a natural birth, prepare for a twin C-section. Even though you are expecting healthy, self-sufficient babies, be ready for twins in the NICU.

There are so many things during a twin pregnancy that fall outside of your control, so you need to focus on what you can control and take each step and surprise as they come. There will be a lot of emotions along the journey. You're absolutely entitled to be mad, angry, sad, and everything in between. This is completely natural. As long as every twist and turn still has your twins on track to arrive healthy and safe, you have reason to rejoice.

The key to surviving any twin pregnancy and delivery is to be flexible. Your babies will arrive on their timeline, and that may not meet your expectations. As many fathers have mentioned to me, you can stay positive in the midst of undesired or unforeseen circumstances by celebrating the successes and positives of each day with your twins. Keep your chin up and be ready for whatever may come.

FROM YOUR FELLOW FATHER OF TWINS...
"One of the things that made it easy for me was actually taking classes with a hospital. Our local hospital here has a program for twin and multiples for the parents to actually go and take the ... 'Hey, this is your first time baby class.' Then we actually got to visit the NICU before anything happened. I think for me that was the most important thing because they said, 'More than likely your kids are going to go in the NICU.' I got to see

what it was like beforehand.

I think one of the most important things that I learned was babies aren't indestructible, but if you're careful with them they're going to be fine. They are fragile, but if you blow on them the wrong way they're not going to explode on you. " - Tim Brien

Chapter Two

Health Care

Do Twins Run in Families?

One of the most frequent questions my wife and I receive when people find out we have twins is, "Do twins run in your family?"

I always want to say, "Yes, they run all over the place now."

Keep in mind that there are two types of twins: identical and fraternal.

Identical Twins

Identical twins are a random occurrence and have no connection to your family history. If you have identical twins, like we did, you can say you won the twin lottery. The odds of having identical twins are about 3 per 1,000 births, regardless of parent's age, race, or family history.

Because identical twins are random, your twins are no more likely than you were to have twins of their own.

Fraternal Twins

Fraternal twins happen when the mother releases two eggs at once and both are fertilized.

There is a genetic disposition in some mothers to hyper-ovulate. This condition can be hereditary.

Dads, your family history has no impact on whether you will have twins. This is true even if you are a fraternal twin or you have a parent who is a fraternal twin. No matter what you do, you can't ovulate and thus any family history of twins is irrelevant.

The odds of having fraternal twins increase when the mother's family has a history of hyper-ovulation and fraternal twins.

Increasing Your Odds

The older the mother is, the more likely she is to release more than one egg, even if she has no family history of twins. Certain fertility drugs also increase your odds of fraternal twins.

Frequent Doctor Visits

Plan for frequent doctor visits during a twin pregnancy. You'll get multiple ultrasounds and checkups during the pregnancy that a normal singleton pregnancy doesn't enjoy.

There are few things that compare to seeing your twin babies on the ultrasound or hearing the two hearts beating on the heartbeat monitor. You don't want to miss these opportunities.

Make arrangements with work and for child care for your other kids so that you can go to the doctor visits with your wife. It will help you support your wife and you'll start to build a bond with your unborn twin babies.

Questions to Ask Your Doctor

Once you find out that you are expecting twins, your mind races with tons of concerns and questions. You'll want to find a good doctor that you can trust and with whom you can have a great relationship. You need to feel comfortable asking any questions you have and asking follow-ups if you still have concerns.

Take some time to brainstorm with your spouse the questions that you have. Write them down and take the list with you to your next doctor visit. This way you won't forget in the moment what you wanted to ask.

Here are some example questions you could ask:

- How will this pregnancy be different from a singleton pregnancy?

- What tests should Mom expect to have during a twin pregnancy?

- What are the frequency and types of doctor visits we should expect throughout this pregnancy?

- How much weight is Mom expected to gain?

- How much more should Mom be eating to support the babies?

- How much water should Mom drink each day?

- Can Mom exercise? What kinds are approved for moms of "high risk" pregnancies?

- When should we expect to feel movement with our twins?

- What are the possible complications with twins and when should we worry?

- What are the chances Mom will have to go on bed rest?

- Are doctor visits based on the actual due date or a more realistic due date (measurements of both Mom and the babies)?

- Will the delivery be based on the actual due date or a more realistic due date?

- What are the signs of pre-term labor we should be looking for?

- What is your experience delivering twins vaginally?

- What is your experience delivering twins via C-section? At how many weeks will you schedule a C-section?

- Do you have rights to deliver at my hospital?

- Does our hospital have at least a Level II NICU?

- How long should we expect to stay in the hospital after delivery, assuming no complications?

Keeping the Twins' Gender a Surprise

You can find out the gender of your babies fairly early in the pregnancy (12-13 weeks). However, the reveal most often happens around 18 weeks.

My wife and I found out as soon as we could what gender our twins were so we could make appropriate preparations. But if you prefer to keep it a surprise, it is possible with some special steps.

One of the challenges that you have in keeping twins' gender a surprise during the pregnancy is that you're going to have a greater number of ultrasounds than you would with a singleton baby. You're going to be in the doctor's office seeing the twins a lot during the pregnancy, and so you may get a peek at identifying features of each baby that reveal it's a boy or it's a girl.

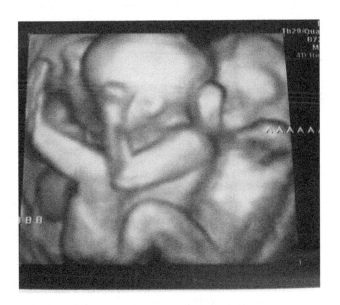

You'll have extra ultrasounds
during her twin pregnancy.

You have to be very cautious in those ultrasounds and make sure that the technician who is doing the ultrasound knows that you want to keep gender a surprise. That way they can use more care when they're moving the wand around on the ultrasound and as they talk to you about what they are seeing.

When do you start feeling the twins move during the pregnancy?

The size of the babies and the location of the placentas all impact when you can feel the babies move. The placentas can act as a buffer between the baby and the outside world.

When you go to see ultrasounds of your twins, you'll see the babies bouncing around all over the place and you'll wonder why you don't feel anything or why mom doesn't feel anything? They look so active!

Mom will start to feel flutters from the twins around 15 to 16 weeks and for sure by around 20 weeks to 24 weeks. If mom has not been pregnant before, she may not know what these flutters feel like and they may be a new experience to her. As the dad on the outside looking in, you're not going to feel them for several weeks later. You should start to feel them from the outside between 22 to 26 weeks along.

I know I loved to see and feel the movements of our twins on my wife's belly but you don't always get that dramatic combination of seeing a kick or a punch through your wife's belly and also feeling that movement on her belly. Sometimes my wife would say, "Hey, put your hand on my belly," and I'd wait, and I'd wait, and I'd wait, and I'd get frustrated that I didn't feel anything.

Be patient because before you know it, mom is going to be complaining of all the intense movement and the dancing and kicking and punching that's going on inside her. And then, dad, you'll definitely be able to feel it from the outside. It will be an exciting milestone!

Handling Pregnancy Complications

Unfortunately, twin pregnancies are often at higher risk than singleton pregnancies for several complications.

The mother can suffer from gestational diabetes, hypertension, or even preterm labor.

Your unborn twins could be monoamniotic, conjoined, or suffer from twin-to-twin transfusion syndrome. There may even be placenta problems or a twin may have unexpected growth restriction issues.

There are numerous possible problems that can afflict your twin pregnancy. It is useful to know about them in case there's anything you can do to prepare or prevent. But if you worry about each of them, you will drive yourself crazy.

Talk to your doctor about how you can prevent the complications you can control, and don't worry about the rest right now. When complications arise, do your homework, talk to your doctor, and deal with the situation as it is.

If you are anxious about any and all possible problems, you won't have the mental or physical energy to focus on what you can do and what you can control.

Hold on to the wisdom of the proverb: "Prepare for the worst, expect the best, and take what comes."

MoDi Twins

Monochorionic diamniotic, or MoDi twins, have two amniotic sacs but share one placenta. This type of pregnancy does have a higher risk of twin-to-twin transfusion syndrome. These twins are always identical.

However, even with the advances of ultrasound technology, sometimes it's hard to tell if there are two placentas or if one has simply fused together. If the twins are the same gender, there's really no way to know just from the ultrasound, if they are MoDi or DiDi twins.

DiDi Twins

Dichorionic diamniotic, or DiDi twins have separate amniotic sacs and two separate placentas. This is the lowest risk of all the twin types of pregnancies. These twins can be either identical or fraternal. If you find out in utero that they are the same sex twins then you'll have to wait until after they are born to determine if they're fraternal or identical.

MoMo Twins

Having twins in the same amniotic sac in mom's uterus is a pretty rare event, occurring in about 1 percent of twin pregnancies. Twins in this circumstance are called monochorionic monoamniotic twins, or MoMo twins.

These twins share a placenta, will always be identical, and have a higher risk of complications. Some of the risks include umbilical cord entanglement or twin-to-twin transfusion syndrome.

Fortunately, even though these twins have a higher risk of complications, they also have a very high successful birth rate.

Take Special Care

If your wife is carrying MoMo twins, odds are she will be on bed rest and may even be checked into the hospital so that the babies can be carefully monitored as the pregnancy progresses. Any complications could cause the babies to be delivered very early. As a result, these twins usually arrive by Caesarian section.

MoMo Twins May Be Misdiagnosed

Many parents who at first hear they have MoMo twins can end up having a different diagnosis when further ultrasounds reveal the thin membrane between the twins' amniotic sacs.

We had a couple of ultrasounds with our twins before they could clearly see the membrane that divided the two amniotic sacs and made it very clear that our girls were not MoMo twins. Even to the trained eye of the medical staff, it was very hard to see that membrane until after several ultrasounds.

FROM YOUR FELLOW FATHER OF TWINS...
"They couldn't find the membrane so there was a risk of having the umbilical cord being wrapped around each

other and my wife would have to be on bed rest for like 20 weeks or even hospitalized. That was really stressful and the doctor went over all the options. Unfortunately, it was during the holiday season and our next appointment wasn't even until the New Year. We had to go through the holiday season wondering about this and it was really really hard for us. Then after two months of not finding the membrane, we went to a specialist who had more high tech equipment. As soon as she put the wand on on my wife's belly, they instantly saw the membrane. We were very relieved about that." - Tim Blaisdell

What is Twin-to-Twin Transfusion Syndrome?

Twin-to-twin transfusion syndrome (TTTS) is one of the extra health concerns that are unique to a twin pregnancy. TTTS occurs only with identical twins while still in the womb. Only monochorionic twins, or those that share a placenta, are susceptible to TTTS. TTTS is a rare condition that happens in only 10-15 percent of identical twin pregnancies.

Due to how abnormal blood vessels form in a shared placenta, TTTS occurs when one twin becomes a "donor" and transfers blood to the other twin (known as the "recipient"). The donor twin will have stunted growth due to a lack of blood and amniotic fluid. The recipient twin will have too much blood and amniotic fluid and subsequent heart trouble.

Why Does TTTS happen?

Why TTTS occurs is largely unknown, but it can occur during any point in the pregnancy and can happen suddenly. Moms often indicate that their belly seemed to grow significantly bigger overnight or they experience rapid weight gain (not due to eating).

Ultrasound Detection

Your doctor will be able to tell early via ultrasounds what types of twins you are expecting and if they share a placenta or not. Due to the complexities of twin pregnancies, Mom will be getting lots of ultrasounds. There will be lots of opportunities to monitor and verify the health of your twins.

Prevention and Treatment

Some research indicates that TTTS can be prevented with certain nutritional plans. A TTTS diagnosis will likely mean bed rest for Mom. Laser surgery can be used in severe cases to prevent further transfer of blood between the twins.

TTTS can lead to serious health issues with your twins and even death. However, the odds are in your favor that it won't happen with your twins. When TTTS does occur, advances in modern medicine allow early diagnosis and highly successful treatment that will likely lead to two healthy babies joining your family.

FROM YOUR FELLOW FATHER OF TWINS...
"When my wife went for her 28-week ultrasound, they found out that she was having contractions, which was

way too early for somebody to be having contractions. We then found out that there was twin-to-twin transfusion syndrome. This hit us like a brick and came out of nowhere. I never even heard of it. It was really to the point where I didn't really realize how common it is for twins to be born early. I thought maybe three weeks early, something like that. I wasn't really worried about that. But when it was at the 28-week mark, it was super scary. It was very risky.

The doctors couldn't give us any answers, and that made it even worse. It was just a lonely kind of feeling of, 'Alright, we got to basically tough this one out.' The whole game plan from there was for my wife to stay in the hospital for as long as possible and try to tough this out and get it to a point where the twins can keep developing and getting to a certain weight and a certain development. They were born at 29 weeks and were in the NICU for 56 days before coming home." - James Bethe

Preeclampsia During the Twin Pregnancy

Preeclampsia is a serious condition that causes extreme high blood pressure in the mother. This, in turn, reduces the blood flow to the placenta and is a dangerous situation for your unborn twins.

Preeclampsia is also known as toxemia or pregnancy-induced hypertension and typically happens during the second half of the twin pregnancy.

Singleton pregnancies experience preeclampsia in only 1 out of 20 cases. Twin pregnancies are at a higher risk with 1 in 5 (or more) experiencing preeclampsia.

Preeclampsia Detection: Symptoms

Warning signs of preeclampsia include a rapid rise in blood pressure, protein in the urine, sudden and disproportionate weight gain, and swelling of the face and hands. At each prenatal visit, your wife's urine will be tested for protein, and thus preeclampsia.

Call your doctor right away if your wife is experiencing any of these symptoms. Don't wait for your next prenatal visit!

Preeclampsia Prevention and Treatment

Like twin-to-twin transfusion syndrome, the causes of preeclampsia aren't very well known. Therefore your focus should be on watching for the symptoms and signs of preeclampsia.

Some sources (like Dr. Luke's *When You're Expecting Twins, Triplets, or Quads*) indicate that eating food or supplements with Omega-3, Calcium, Vitamin C, and Vitamin E may help prevent preeclampsia. However, the important thing is to learn the warning signs (described above) and consult your physician if you suspect problems.

Typical treatments for preeclampsia include bed rest and modification to your wife's diet (more water, less salt). In extreme cases, your wife may need to be hospitalized.

Preeclampsia is ultimately cured when the babies are born. Unfortunately, this means your babies may be born early if the preeclampsia cannot be treated effectively.

Dad's Role

- Make sure your wife gets regular prenatal visits. Go with her if you can.
- Watch for the symptoms of preeclampsia like swelling of the hands and face and sudden and rapid weight gain.
- When in doubt, call your wife's doctor (or help her do so).
- If preeclampsia strikes, be ready to help your wife during bed rest and possibly deal with premature twins.

FROM YOUR FELLOW FATHER OF TWINS... "My wife had preeclampsia. Her last month of the pregnancy she was on bed rest. What made that even more difficult was I worked about an hour away. At the time I had a strict Monday through Friday job and having her an hour away with the slightest little sign or symptom popping up was kind of difficult, emotionally and mentally for me. I was looking at my phone constantly waiting for a call from her, if she needed anything or if she was feeling bad." - Steve Smith

How Early Can Twins Be Born?

Twins are usually born an average of four weeks early
because there's not much space in the womb.

Twins can be born much earlier than singleton births. It's possible to deliver twins after less than 25 weeks of pregnancy. The earlier twins are born, the higher their risk of developing multiple health problems.

On average, twins are delivered after 36 weeks of gestation. Contrast that with the average for non-twins: 40 weeks. In other words, twins tend to be delivered a full month earlier than non-twins. Our twin girls were delivered at 36 weeks.

Why Are Twins Born so Early?

Twins are delivered earlier than non-twins largely because of decreased space in the womb. There simply isn't enough room in the womb for twins to grow to the size of singleton babies before birth.

A lot depends on whether the twins are sharing the same placenta or each twin has its own placenta. Twins that share the same placenta are called monochorionic twins. Twins that do not share placentas are called dichorionic twins.

Monochorionic twins have a much higher risk of having problems during pregnancy than dichorionic twins. They typically have shorter gestation times than dichorionic twins.

Monochorionic twins do not always share the placenta equally. Sometimes, like in the case of twin-to-twin transfusion syndrome one twin receives a lot more blood and oxygen than the other. Because babies that are dichorionic twins have their own placentas, they do not have any placenta-related blood flow problems.

Survival Rates

Survival rates for twins depend on how long their gestation period is and their birth weight. The longer the gestation period, the better the survival rates. The lower the birth weight, the worse the survival rates.

Roughly half of all twins can be classified as low birth weight, 5 lbs. 7 oz. (2,500 grams) or less. Survival rates for twins between 3 lbs. 5 oz. and 4 lbs. 7 oz. (1,500 to 2,000

grams) are quite good. They can be as high as 95 percent, surprising as this might seem.

On the other hand, survival rates for twins less than 2 lbs.
3 oz. (1,000 grams) are only 70 percent. That can be frighten-
ing to a lot of prospective parents.

Fortunately, the vast majority of twins have a birth weight
greater than 2 lbs. 3 oz. when they are delivered. Most parents
of twins do not need to worry about their twins being born
with birth weights this low.

Maximizing Twins' Chances

The mother's lifestyle can make a real difference. Women
pregnant with twins who do their best to remain in excellent
health during pregnancy are less likely to deliver early than
pregnant women with poor health.

Pregnant women can help their babies by avoiding smok-
ing and alcohol. A healthy diet rich in fruits and vegetables
also helps diminish the risk of complications with pregnancy.

Be sure to consult with your physician for specific advice
on your twin pregnancy.

A Secret to Full-Term Twins

Our obstetrician told my wife to plan to rest for at least an
hour each morning and afternoon with her feet up after she
hit the second trimester. As the pregnancy progressed, that
recommended rest time expanded. Our doctor cited studies

that showed conclusive evidence that daily rest time with feet up helped increase the odds of carrying twins to term.

You can increase your odds of a full-term twin pregnancy by making sure Mommy gets off her feet and rests.

This may look different in each family situation. We were grateful we received this advice early in our pregnancy so we had time to make plans and provisions for the second and third trimesters before they arrived.

Support Your Wife During Bed Rest

A twin pregnancy is significantly more likely to result in bed rest for the mother. After all, Mom is carrying two babies and will not only be uncomfortably large as the pregnancy progresses, but she is at higher risk for the other pregnancy complications we've discussed.

While on bed rest during the twin pregnancy, your wife will need emotional and physical support. Ideally, you'll be giving her that support. If you are not able to help as much as is required (perhaps due to work commitment or related travel), you need to get helpers.

Emotional Support

- *Empathy* – Your wife will be going through something that you'll never experience. Nevertheless, you need to listen to her and let her share her feelings with you so you can better support her during this challenging time.

- *Words* – Yes, Dad, you'll need to verbalize your thoughts and feelings in support of your wife. Talk with her and encourage her during the bed rest.

Our older boys made it tough for my wife to rest.

- *Comfort Items* – Your wife will want some things (food, entertainment, etc.) that will help her feel better emotionally. Identify and deliver those comfort items your wife likes.

- *Manifest in Actions* – All the words in the world won't mean a thing if you don't take action and show your wife you mean what you say. Take action and actually serve your wife in her moments of need.

Physical Support

- *Priorities* – Your wife's health and the health of your unborn twins are your first priority. Look at the bed rest situation through that perspective and opportunities to help your wife will become obvious.

- *Remove Burdens* – When your wife is on bed rest with the twins, you must remove as many of her burdens as possible. Consider shouldering the responsibilities of everything she does around the house. Look around; is there something that needs to be done? Do it.

- *Comfort* – I hurt just watching my wife during the later stages of the twin pregnancy. It didn't seem physically possible for her to be carrying two babies and still be able to function. Your wife will be extremely uncomfortable. Do everything you can to make her comfortable. Let her rest. Bring her what she needs. Massage her swollen feet.

FROM YOUR FELLOW FATHER OF TWINS...
"I put cribs together. I put rockers together. I helped my wife stay off her feet as much as possible. I did dinner and dishes. I did everything I could to make sure she was comfortable. I tried to take care of all the odds and ends and keep her off her feet and as comfortable as possible." - Jonathan Blundell

Survive Bed Rest with a Plan

Bed rest for your wife means no rest for you. The key to help-ing your wife survive bed rest during your twin pregnancy is to identify everything she does during the day and find a sub-stitute.

Child Care

As a stay-at-home mom, my wife's primary responsibility dur-ing the day was to care for our two preschool-age boys. To help alleviate the toll of child care, we called in helpers every day. Friends with similarly aged kids came over for morning play dates. When our boys napped, my wife would nap. We paid a babysitter three afternoons a week to play with our sons so my wife could rest. I arranged my work schedule so I could go home a little earlier two afternoons a week to help with the boys.

It will require a bit of planning and sacrifice, but it's possi-ble to make arrangements for child care at minimal cost.

You may have other options available to you, like hiring a nanny or having family members close by who can help with child care. Get creative and do what will work best for your family.

Food Preparation

We stocked our freezer with ready-to-cook meals. This helped reduce time in the kitchen and let others (i.e., me) quickly prepare meals for the family. Our church group also gener-ously brought us meals over the course of my wife's bed rest.

Creativity is a key here, as well. If you're not a friend to the freezer section at the supermarket, maybe collecting take-out menus is more your style. Order double your normal fare and freeze the leftovers. Don't forget to label your containers so you know what is in your freezer.

Use the time during the first trimester to double recipes when doing normal cooking so you can stock your freezer gradually. If you don't need to resort to using freezer meals during bed rest, most certainly you'll use them during the early months of twin babyhood.

Cleaning

With twins, you'll need to reset your expectations of a clean house. A bed rest pregnancy helps you face that reality even before your twins are born.

During our twin pregnancy, we had friends come over and help clean, paid some teenagers to clean other times, and even had our preschoolers step up and help.

Transportation

If Mom is the taxi in your family, you'll need a different driver. Consider carpools with others for activities. You may even want to adjust your work schedule if needed so you can pick up kids or run the errands that your wife normally handles.

Work

For the expectant mother, working while pregnant with twins is an extra challenge on top of caring for home and family. If your work is more flexible than your wife's job, adjust your schedule to help fill in the gaps previously discussed. Encourage your wife to seek alternative work options that allow her to stay off her feet.

Eventually the time will come to leave work to finish the pregnancy and deliver the babies. Remember that under the Family and Medical Leave Act in the United States, both the mother and father can use up to 12 weeks of leave for prenatal and post-pregnancy care. Your company will likely have specific policies on how that time is allocated (vacation vs. sick time or time without pay).

You may decide to use your time off in different blocks rather than all at once. The fact is that your family needs you at home for more time than you can take off work, so you must be smart about when to use it. When our twins were born, I took a week off work. Most of that time was spent in the hospital, but it did give me a few days back home with our newborn girls.

I then returned to work for several months because we had lined up helpers to come and stay with us. When all our helpers went home, I then took the last piece of my paternity leave. That way we were able to extend as long as possible the time my wife had someone with her to help with the kids.

Make Your List

Make a list of everything your wife does during the day around the house, at work, or in the community.

Review the list and decide what can be cut. A twin pregnancy will require that some activities be dropped until a post-delivery time. With each item, ask, "Does this absolutely have to happen each day?" and "What is the worst that will happen if this doesn't get done?"

Take what is left on the list and write the names of people who can help with those items. It may be you, it may be a neighbor, a friend, a family member, or someone from your church group.

Take Action

Remember that when people say, "If there is anything I can do to help, just let me know," this is your chance to enlist helpers. These people will be invaluable to you as you deal with bed rest. Don't be afraid to ask for help and commit people to specific things they can do to help you. If you make your list as outlined above, you'll know exactly where these well-wishers can help out.

You want your twins to continue growing in the safety of Mommy's womb for as long as possible. Her job is to grow healthy babies. Your job is to do whatever it takes to let her do her job. Do everything you can to let your wife rest, and you'll significantly increase your odds of avoiding premature twins.

WHAT MOM IS FEELING: "Exhaustion. I couldn't believe how debilitating carrying multiples would be. I spent several months on bed rest, and it was worth every second of it: 2 healthy girls born 37 weeks, 6.8 and 6.10 pounds." - Victoria Tiedt

Picking a Pediatrician for your Twins

Our children's pediatrician came as a recommendation from my wife's doctor and later from some friends. Regardless of how you find a pediatrician, you'll want to make sure they are a good fit for your family.

Many pediatricians have open-house style meetings where you can go and meet with the doctor, office staff, and nurses. See if you like the location, office, and the personality of the staff before you decide to pick them as the pediatrician for your kids.

Look for a pediatrician who is experienced with twins or multiples. If a pediatrician has been in practice for any amount of time, she should have already had exposure to twins and multiples as a matter of course. However, you'll want to ask specifically about twins. If the pediatrician dismisses twins as if they're just two singletons, you might want to look elsewhere. You want a doctor to acknowledge the fact that twins are unique.

You want to have a doctor's office that will let you have simultaneous appointments for your twins, not necessarily back to back. You want to be able to have two appointments in one sitting so you don't have to go back to the doctor later.

Look for a board-certified pediatrician which means he or she has gone through extra training and ongoing certification in Pediatrics. It will give you a doctor with an extra level of knowledge and experience. Doctors can be board certified in lots of different specialties so you want to look for a board-certified pediatrician who will meet your needs.

Double check your insurance to see if the pediatrician who you like to take your kids to is actually on your insurance plan and in your network so that your out-of-pocket expenses will be reduced.

Week by Week Twin Pregnancy Guide

For a week by week twin pregnancy guide, visit: dadsguidetotwins.com/extras

Each week outlines what to expect, fetal development, symptoms and health conditions, what to prepare at this time, and how things should be progressing in your twin pregnancy.

Chapter Three

Preparing Your Family

There's Room in Your Heart for Twins

If you already have a child before your twins, you may wonder, "How can I love more children as much as I love my current child?"

As you begin the parenthood journey, you grow to love your first child and ultimately can't imagine life without this son or daughter in your family. As time passes, you start to forget what life was like before this little one joined your home.

Then you find out you are expecting your next child—or two. When our second son was born, I wondered how I could love him as much as his older brother. What kind of relationship would I have with him? How would that compare to the relationship I had with his brother?

You may think it will be hard to love two babies at once,
but your ability to love expands to include them both.

Fortunately, there is an amazing phenomenon of parenting that I don't think is unique to twins. The magic is that your ability to love expands to cover all the new children that join your family. You may have heard this from others before, and it's true! Look forward to experiencing the magic yourself.

I love my firstborn as much as my fourth child. At each point that a new baby joined our family, I wondered how it would work. And yet, it did. I instantly fell in love with each of my kids when I first saw them in the delivery room.

Twins offer a unique experience to their fathers. With twins, you need to love not just their older sibling(s) but both babies at the same time.

Nevertheless, the magic of parenting still happens, and your love will expand to cover both your newborn twin babies.

I think the fact that most twins come early and are smaller than singleton babies makes them even more endearing to you as a father. You can't help but reach out to them and want to love and support them in their fragile, newborn state.

Creative Ways to Announce a Twin Pregnancy

There are many creative ways to announce a twin pregnancy. Since most of your friends and family won't be expecting the surprise news that you are having twins, you can have some fun when you announce you're expecting twins.

While you'll find many creative ways to announce a pregnancy by searching online, most are relevant to singleton babies. Maybe hearing the way we announced our twin pregnancy will help get your creative juices flowing.

We bought two identical picture frames that hold 3"x5" size photos. For each picture frame, we printed off a picture of baby feet. In the first frame, we put the words, "Save this space for me" over the picture. In the second frame, we had the words: "And me too."

We wrapped both frames up together as a gift and gave them to the grandparents. Since we found out we were having twins on Christmas Eve, a gift wasn't an unusual thing to receive. However, if you want to announce your twins some other time, the gift idea will still work. Everyone loves to get a present!

When the grandparents unwrapped the gift, the first impression was, "Oh, what beautiful picture frames!"

Then they read the words and realized we were announcing our pregnancy. They asked, "Are you pregnant?" Their happy response was brief as they tried to mentally process why they were holding two picture frames.

After a brief pause, they figured out the second picture frame, and expressions of shock overcame their faces. "You're having twins?!"

It was a fun process to watch as the grandparents, other family members, and friends slowly uncovered the announcement of our twin pregnancy.

I managed to discreetly video record their reactions, and it is a blast to go back and watch these.

Remember, when you announce your twin pregnancy, people will be completely shocked. Enjoy the moment and plan a creative announcement that fosters great memories of the experience.

Here are some other announcement ideas to try:

- A 2-for-1 deal, or buy one get one free

- Double — double the fun, double dip, double your family size (if the twins are your first babies), seeing double, double trouble
- Babies: So good you can't have just one
- 20 fingers, 20 toes, four eyes, four legs, or other multiple body parts (as in our family is growing by four feet!)
- Mom is a little "two" good at pregnancy, or Mom is an overachiever
- Comes with a built-in friend, a tennis partner, a backup, a stunt double

FROM YOUR FELLOW FATHER OF TWINS... "We had let everybody know that we were pregnant but nobody knew that it was going to be twins. For my wife's birthday party, I went online and found a company that made fortune cookies with custom tape inside. I had them write that we were expecting twins and everybody opened that and went crazy. Then it was 'oh, what are you having?' The first one we did a scratch off that reveals either a pink or a blue onesie. Everybody scratched off and saw the pink one and then the second one we had a box with balloons in it and we opened up the box and there were pink balloons saying it's a girl and again everybody went crazy." - Adam Ross

Preparing Your Marriage

Any pregnancy and newborn arrival is a trial for a marriage. Time and energy is taken away from each other and focused on the baby. Unless you are prepared, this can catch you off guard and could potentially damage your relationship with your wife.

When twins are in the mix, things get really complicated. Your wife will likely be miserable for a large chunk of the pregnancy. She will be physically uncomfortable, mentally exhausted, and emotionally spent.

In this frazzled state of mind, she will say something, do something, or even forget something that will make you feel frustrated, mad, angry, sad, or just forgotten.

Survival Tip #1: Don't take it personally.

Remember your loving and adoring wife from pre-pregnancy. She will be back. You just need to hang in there for a few months.

This season of misery will pass. Every pregnancy comes to an end. Your twins can only stay in there so long before they come out. Be patient, especially with your wife.

Survival Tip #2: Forget yourself and get to work.

A twin pregnancy is not the time to be selfish or needy. Put the needs of your wife and unborn twins ahead of your own.

If you focus on their needs, you won't have time to think about all the things you used to do that you no longer have time to enjoy. You will find your love for your twins growing because of your unselfish service.

Survival Tip #3: Talk to your wife before the rough times.

Talk things over with your wife at the beginning of the pregnancy.

Acknowledge that things may get rough for a time but that you are both committed to seeing it through. Work out some phrases you can use with each other to help smooth over tense moments when they arise.

Think of your twin pregnancy as preparation for the marital trial that awaits you after the kids are born.

Double newborns will introduce a whole new level of life interruption and demands that will put you in mere survival mode. In survival mode, there is no time for your spouse unless you make time for it.

Keep your marriage alive during the zombie-like weeks of newborn twins by taking advantage of the small moments to connect with each other. A small touch, a helping hand, a kind word, a quick shoulder rub or another sign of affection can mean the world to the frazzled postpartum mommy.

And although it isn't part of our nature, it's important that we as dads identify small things that will be meaningful to us and communicate those to our wives. It's likely that your wife will feel guilty over the burden that's been placed on you as Super Dad and she will want to know ways she can nurture you as well.

Survival Tip #4: Make some alone time.

There will be a lack of marital intimacy after the twins are born. In due time, the physical demands of newborn twins will ease up and you can get back in your routine. As with getting out of the house, you'll likely want to schedule alone time with your wife too or it won't happen.

As soon as your twins start to fall into a predictable pattern of feeding and sleeping, you need to plan a date with your wife. This date may just be an hour away from the house to run an errand or go out to eat. Nevertheless, be sure to schedule this time or it will never happen. Getting a babysitter for your twins isn't too hard if you do a little prep work.

Your marriage can and will survive newborn twins. Set clear expectations with each other. Take every opportunity to spend time together. Actively work on your relationship and it will come out stronger than ever.

WHAT   MOM   IS   FEELING...
"Although this was my fifth pregnancy, there was little to do to prepare for how absolutely exhausting it is to grow two humans in your belly. By dinner time I was too exhausted and nauseous to cook most nights. Be prepared for a lot of take out, crock pot meals, or for dad to do a lot of the cooking!" - Brandi Khoury

Sleeping With a Pregnant Lady

Don't expect to get great sleep for the duration of your wife's pregnancy. Some twin moms end up kicking daddy out of the bed so they can sprawl out and get more comfortable during the later stages of the pregnancy.

If you are lucky enough to still be allowed in the same bed for the entire gestation, prepare yourself for abnormal sleeping arrangements. As your wife progresses in the pregnancy, she will have a more and more difficult time getting comfortable and sleeping. You may have to run and get her antacids in the middle of the night.

Your bed will likely be overflowing with pillows as she tries to prop up or support different parts of her body. If you hear moans or groaning in middle of the night, it is just your wife trying to roll over or get out of bed.

My advice? Be sympathetic ... and get a pair of earplugs.

W H A T   M O M   I S   F E E L I N G . . .
"In the early days, even before I knew I was expecting twins, I was really, really tired. And, once I got bigger, finding a comfortable sleeping position was tough. I used a giant u-shaped pillow, which enabled me to shift from side to side with support, but quality sleep was pretty much out from about 6 months on. Guess it's your body's way of preparing you for life without sleep with two newborns!" - Meredith Rhodes

Sex During a Twin Pregnancy

Sex is usually very safe during a pregnancy. However, things get complicated when your wife starts getting very large and uncomfortable. So while technically, your doctor may approve of sex during the pregnancy, your wife will likely be too exhausted, uncomfortable, and even lack the desire for it during the majority of the pregnancy.

Knowing this, make sex one of the topics you discuss early in the pregnancy. Talk about ways you can still connect physically and emotionally even when your wife isn't in the mood for sex.

Also keep in mind that sex is often mentioned as a way to kick-start labor at the end of a pregnancy. You definitely don't want this to happen prematurely, so don't get too crazy in the later stages of pregnancy, especially if your wife is on bed rest.

Nagging

You need to be your wife's watchdog or manager, someone who makes sure she is taking care of herself and the babies. Sometimes, some gentle nagging on your part is required.

Your doctor will outline certain things your wife needs to do to stay healthy. Make sure your wife follows these instructions and is eating properly, staying hydrated, and is getting the rest she needs.

If your wife is anything like mine, she will probably act like she didn't hear the doctor and keep on doing the things she does to take care of the household. She's trying to avoid feeling guilty about not pulling her load when she takes time to rest and takes extra care of herself.

Agree ahead of time how you will remind her and help her so that when she hears your promptings, she knows you're trying to help and not just harping on her.

How to Prepare Older Kids for Twins

Sometimes twins are not your first children. You need to prepare your older children for the arrival of their twin siblings.

My wife and I had two sons before our twin girls arrived. At the time our twins were born, the boys were 3 and almost 2 years old, respectively. I knew that life would be different once the girls were born, but I didn't really understand how that would impact their brothers.

Here are some things that helped us get our older kids ready and helped them survive the twins' arrival.

Help Kids Get Excited

Get your other kids ready for your twins' arrival by making it real and personal for them.

We started telling our boys that Mommy was expecting early on in the pregnancy. As soon as we knew the twins were girls, we started to refer to them as "sisters" when talking with our boys.

Toward the end of the pregnancy, we had decided on names and started calling the unborn twins by those names. Our boys knew the names and started referring to the babies by name, too. They completely understood that Mommy was going to have two babies.

Tell Kids What to Expect

We talked a lot with our boys about what would happen when the babies were born. We outlined who would come and take care of them and that Mommy and Daddy would be in the hospital for a few days.

Our boys were excited to meet their sisters because
we had been talking to them about the twins' arrival.

We even did role playing with our boys. We practiced together how to hold a baby doll, how to be gentle with a baby, and taught them what it meant when a baby was crying. We showed them where the diapers, blankets, and burp cloths were in the house. We had them practice finding the diapers and bringing them to Mommy when she asked so they'd be ready to help.

Children's Books to Help Prepare Siblings

Words and discussions can only go so far in these preparations. I read a couple of books about twins with our kids and they liked them. They are written from the perspective of the older sibling. In fact, the author, Paris Morris, was the older sibling when her twin siblings arrived. Each book walks through what the older sibling is seeing, feeling, and thinking and how the twins fit in with her life.

I'm Having Twins explores a 3-year-old girl's adjustment to the reality that twins will be joining her family. View the twin pregnancy through her eyes and see how she comes to terms with the twins' pending arrival.

My Twins are Coming Home focuses on Paris' experience once her twin sisters were born: seeing them in the NICU, waiting for them to come home, dealing with their arrival, and so on.

These books are short and fully illustrated and will fit nicely with your other children's books.

Make the Moment Special for Them

You may want to have a small gift for the older sibling(s) tucked away in your hospital bag. When they come to meet their new babies, you can give them the gift and tell them it's from the babies, who are so excited to have them for an older brother or sister.

It's also a nice way to acknowledge the older child and give them the spotlight for a moment or two.

Arrange Help

You will need to have plans in place for someone to come and take care of your children. These plans should include short-term and long-term plans.

Because my wife was on partial bed rest, we had to bring in help well before delivery. At first, our boys were reluctant to have someone come over. Over time, they warmed up to our friends and got used to having helpers with them at our house. This was vital in setting the stage for post-delivery.

When your wife goes into labor, you need to have a short list of people you can call who will immediately come over and stay with your current children. It is vital that these people are those your kids know and trust. That means that they should already be interacting with your kids leading up to delivery.

Once the babies arrive, you will need to switch over to longer-term help. You will need someone who can stay with you, and if not that, at least come and help you every day. This person may simply take care of your other children while you and your wife care for the twins. Or alternatively, you can spend one-on-one time with your older children while your helper cares for a baby.

As we were preparing for the arrival of our twins, we had several parents of twins tell us, "GET HELP!" Because of that, we arranged for individual family members and friends to come and stay with us over the course of the first two months after our twins were born. This was one of the best decisions we ever made for our family. It not only helped us as parents survive but allowed our older kids to get some attention during this transition time as well, both from us and from others.

When to Bring the Kids for a Hospital Visit

When our twins were born, we took a day in the hospital to recover before bringing the kids over. My wife had gone through a C-section to deliver the twins and needed some time to physically recover.

Since every twin pregnancy and delivery is different, don't commit to any visitors until the twins are born and you've settled down in the hospital. Last minute complications can arise that will squash any firm plans.

If your twins go to the NICU, be sure to reset expectations with their siblings. Your other children need to know that their new twin babies will be hooked up to lots of machines and that they won't be able to hold or touch the twins.

To younger kids, a hospital room is like a playground. There are so many things to discover and climb on (like the fully adjustable hospital bed) that you'll need to at least do a first pass at kid proofing the hospital room. Dad, this is your job since your wife will still be recovering physically. Tidy up before your kids arrive to meet their twin siblings or you'll spend the entire visit trying to keep your kids out of trouble.

How Will My Toddler React to the Twins?

Our two sons reacted differently to the arrival of their twin sisters. Our older boy loved being around his little sisters and he enjoyed helping as much as a 3-year-old could help. The younger boy basically ignored his little sisters after the initial excitement wore off. It took a while for him to warm back up to his sisters. You'll likely see different reactions from your older children too.

So how will your twins affect your toddler? Look for other behaviors of your toddler right now for indications of what you might expect:

- Does your toddler always cling to you?

- Does your toddler always have to be near you? When you leave the room, what happens?

- Is your toddler fine with other family members or around strangers?

- In play groups, at church, or with cousins, how does your toddler handle other little kids?

- If you don't pay attention to your toddler, what happens?

- Can your toddler entertain himself or herself without supervision? Or do you always have to be providing activities and things for them to do?

Ideally, you would be able to foster more independence and self-reliance in your toddler now so that when your twins come and you know you will not have as much time to dedicate to your toddler, the transition will go a little more smoothly. If your toddler already knows how to play, entertain, and take care of himself, then when you are busy with the twins, the whole house won't fall apart.

Be Ready

By keeping your older children as involved as possible during the twin pregnancy, the transition to a suddenly larger family will be that much easier. The younger your older children are, the less likely they will fully understand what is about to happen. You don't even fully understand what twins will mean until they arrive. So err on the side of too many preparations and your mind can be put at ease.

How to Involve the Grandparents

Once your parents find out that you are having twins, they will want to help. Depending on your parents' style, that may be forceful help or more subtle.

When grandparents want to help you, they might not know how to do that. Perhaps they've had grandkids before but twins may be a completely new challenge for them.

Have frank and open conversations with your parents and ask how they would like to help and discuss what help you need.

Supplies

Twins require a lot of baby supplies. Diapers, wipes, clothes, bottles, blankets, cribs, car seats, etc. If the grandparents are financially able, ask them to help stock your home ahead of the babies' arrival.

Child Care

The early days of twins will be a physically demanding time. An extra set of helping hands will greatly ease your burden. Invite your grandparents to come over and help care for the babies. Ask if they can stay the night and take turns caring for the babies while you sleep. Balance the grandparent's physical capabilities and limits with what you ask them to do.

If you have other children in your family, they will need special attention when the twins are born. Grandparents are great candidates to help take care of your older children. Grandparents should already have a relationship of trust with your kids so it is easier to leave them together.

Visiting Grandparents

Getting out of the house to go visit the grandparents is extremely difficult. You'll find that on a Saturday you had planned to visit the grandparents, your twins are not on schedule, things are going crazy, and you're just not going to make it out of the house.

Even though you make plans to visit, those plans may change last minute. It's fine to talk about that reality with your parents and help set those expectations. If you can't get out of the house, it's always great to invite your parents or the in-laws over to see you. This way, they'll get a little glimpse of the reality of life in your house and appreciate your challenges.

Support

Grandparents need to support you in whatever decisions you make as new parents of twins. Parenting twins often requires unorthodox methods that might be foreign to grandparents. Just because they did it one way, doesn't mean you have to do it that way.

Grandparents are attracted to newborn grandkids like a magnet to metal. This can lead to problems with too much grandparent time. You may want some space to establish your family routine. Be sure to clearly discuss your desires to the grandparents.

How You Should Respond to 'If You Need Any Help' Comments

Once your friends and family find out you're having twins, you'll be bombarded with congratulations and many comments like, "If you need any help, please let me know."

As a twin parent, you need help. There isn't any "if" about it. Part of your preparations for your babies should be arranging as much help as possible before your twins arrive.

Many people will offer to help. Instead of just saying "OK, thanks," you need to take action.

Go find or buy a magnetic notepad and put it on the fridge. Whenever anyone says to you, "Let me know if I can help," tell them, "Just a minute!" and go get the pad.

Write down their name, phone number, and ways they are willing to help.

Housework? Babysitting? Bringing in a meal?

You'll be able to gauge their sincerity at wanting to help, and you'll have a fallback for the times when you desperately need help but can't remember in your sleep-deprived, frazzled state of mind who said they were available.

If you have friends or family members who are absolutely sincere and insistent on helping, commit them to taking one overnight shift a week so they can feed the twins when they wake in the middle of the night. Yes, it's an act of love to give you a full night's sleep, one you'll undoubtedly be indebted to them for. But it's one you'll need and be immensely grateful for. This will also be one of the best gifts you can give your wife, who is not only sleep-deprived, but also recovering from a twin pregnancy and possibly a C-section.

Get ready now. Pin down your friends and family on what they can specifically do to help you.

Once the twin babies arrive, you'll be glad you've got help lined up. It's much easier to call someone and say, "Thanks for being available to help, but we're doing okay today," than to need help desperately and not be able to find any.

Chapter Four

Preparing Financially

Twins Require Financial Changes

Twins are not cheap. Your current lifestyle will have to change to adapt financially and prepare for twins.

Consider changing your current budget to increase allotments for diapers, clothing, food, and doctor visits.

Look at what you spend money on every month and see what you can drop to help pay for the twins. Do you really need all those cable television channels? What could you sell on eBay or Craigslist to raise money for a new crib?

You Don't Need a Bigger House

When I first learned we were having twins, I was in shock. I stayed in that state of shock for at least several weeks.

This shock was fueled by fears and questions of how I would successfully care for my family.

Avoid moving during the pregnancy if you can.

One of my big concerns was how my new, bigger family would fit into our current home. I spent several days looking at new house listings and running numbers through mortgage calculators online.

Did we end up buying a new home? No, and you shouldn't either.

Why? If you want to live a long, happy life, don't make a pregnant woman, especially one pregnant with twins, move her family and house.

Your wife will get extremely large with twins. This means possible bed rest and definite exhaustion. Think for a minute about how she might handle packing up the house, moving to a new location, and getting settled into a new place.

Moving is stressful even without a pregnancy. So don't do it. The good news is that you can wait until the babies arrive and reassess the situation.

Amazingly, twins don't initially take up much more space than a singleton baby. Until the twins start getting mobile, you can survive in your current home, assuming you have space for one baby. Twins share a bath, changing table, rocking chair, and even a blanket for tummy time on the floor.

Take a deep breath. Stop searching for a new house. You'll have plenty of new expenses anyway. Why add a bigger mortgage to the list?

Baby-Proofing Can Wait

You may be tempted to baby-proof your entire house during the pregnancy. Don't be in such a hurry.

When you bring your newborns home, they won't immediately run over to the power outlet and stick their finger in it. You'll have several months after the kids are home before you'll need to worry about baby-proofing anything.

If you've already made all your preparations and have extra time during the pregnancy, then start baby-proofing. Otherwise, put this task at the bottom of your to-do list.

You May Not Need a Bigger Car

After worrying about your home, your next thought will be about your car. How are you going to transport your new twins and your current family around town?

Do you need a new car? Here is the simple formula:

Current Number of Kids + Twins + Parents + Future Kid Plans = How many seats you need in your car

If the number of seats you need in a car is greater than what you currently have in your vehicle, it is time to start shopping.

Before we had any kids, I swore that we'd never own a minivan. I told myself and wife that we'd just get a big SUV to haul around the expanding family.

That plan worked until we had two kids. At that point we knew we wanted room to grow and so bought a minivan. Don't feel bad if you have to take back a similar "no minivan" promise. They aren't so bad after all.

So when we found out we were having twins, we already had room in our van and didn't need to buy a new car. However, the girls' arrival immediately maxed out our seating space.

Remember the formula above. If twins are your first kids and you have a back seat in your car, you may be fine waiting to buy a bigger vehicle. If, on the other hand, you already have a child and are driving a little Honda Civic, it is probably time to upgrade.

Keep in mind that car seats are often wider than a normal person. So just because you have three seat belts in the back seat doesn't mean you can fit three car seats back there. Take your car seats to the car dealership when you test drive to make sure they will fit.

What to Stock Up On Before the Twins Arrive

You know that you'll need a lot of stuff to be ready for twins. Once your twins arrive, the last thing that you'll want to do — or have time to do — is go to the store. The solution? Stock up on everything.

"Everything" consists of two categories: stuff your twins will use daily and things that the rest of the family will consume regularly.

Things for the Twins

Stockpiling a little bit here and there will be less of a shock for your budget later.

In addition to all the reusable baby gear that you'll need (strollers, clothing, cribs, etc.), you'll need to stock supplies that your babies will use on a daily basis:

- diapers of all sizes
- baby wipes
- burp cloths

- baby formula
- bottles and nipples
- Desitin or zinc oxide diaper rash cream
- baby body wash/shampoo

Things for the Household

When you think about the household items you use every day, you'll get an idea of the little things that you need to stock up on before the twins come:

- toilet paper
- paper towels
- soap
- dish washing detergent
- shampoo
- deodorant
- toothpaste
- laundry detergent
- dryer sheets

These are things you don't want to worry about for a least a month after the twins arrive.

If you have a stockpile of supplies by the time you hit the third trimester with your twins, you can relax a little as you enjoy the calm before the storm.

The Ideal Baby Shower

Even if you have another child or children, you can still benefit from a twin baby shower. When you have twins, you break a lot of the "normal" rules of having kids (beyond just the obvious two-at-one-time thing). This gives you some liberty with all aspects of the pregnancy, including asking for another baby shower.

Evaluate your circles of friends. Each of those could be a potential baby shower: work, neighbors, church, extended family, etc. And don't be afraid to suggest to a close friend that you might benefit from a twin baby shower.

Plan for your twin baby shower before the end of the second trimester; somewhere around 26 to 28 weeks. You definitely want to have it by 30 to 31 weeks at the latest, because you want to get that baby shower out of the way before Mom is on bed rest or the twins arrive early.

If a kind soul offers to give you a baby shower, ask that it be a frozen meal shower. Most baby showers produce cute clothes and maybe some diapers. If you're lucky, you'll have a few people actually shop using your registry. While all of these things are necessary, let's face it, they don't directly help you, the twin dad. A frozen meal shower may sound a little odd, but it's very worth it.

Guests can either buy something in the frozen food section of the grocery store and gift it to you, or they can make something homemade and bring it to you to freeze for later.

If adequate storage space in your freezer is a concern, it's worth addressing in one way or another. Do you have funds and space to buy an extra freezer? If not, do you have a friend or two nearby who could store some freezer meals for you?

Having a freezer full of food was a lifesaver for us when our twins arrived. It was one of the primary reasons we made it through the first three to four months post-partum. (Not that we had that many meals stored, but every meal lasted our little family 2-3 days!)

A freezer full of food comes in very handy.

The frozen meal shower is a twin dad's best friend. A freezer meal is something that even you, Dad, can cook. Once the twins arrive, both you and your wife will be so exhausted you won't be able to think straight. You need to make sure you are eating well. Skip all the food preparations and throw the frozen meal in the oven or microwave. Problem solved.

You won't eat well unless you are ready. Stock the freezer now!

Free and Cheap Baby Formula

If you decide to formula-feed your baby twins instead of breastfeeding, the costs can add up quickly.

Formula is not cheap and you'll need to try different brands and "flavors" to see what works best with your babies.

The good news is that you don't have to buy every ounce of formula your babies drink. Here are some free and discounted resources:

*Free and cheap baby formula works
just as well as the full-priced stuff.*

Hospital

The hospital where your twins are born has an almost infinite supply of formula. They even have the premixed, liquid versions which are super easy: just pop on a nipple and feed the baby.

Before you leave the hospital, ask for extra samples and stock up. If you've been nice to your nurses during your stay, they will most likely help you out here. It doesn't hurt that you've got twins and they will feel sympathetic to your situation.

Pediatrician

You'll be visiting the pediatrician frequently in the first few weeks and months after your twins' birth. Ask your pediatrician for samples every time you visit.

Also ask your pediatrician for a form you can fill out and mail to the formula company. The formula company will send you a free case of formula. This is one of the perks of having twins. The formula companies want to send you samples, because once you're hooked, they know you'll be buying double the formula.

Manufacturer

Most formula manufacturers have programs where you can sign up for coupons. Take advantage of this. Sure, they will market to you but it is worth the cost savings.

You'll also see discounted formula at wholesale clubs like Costco (another twin dad's best friend) where the manufacturers offer larger sizes at cheaper prices than other grocery or retail stores.

Friends

Odds are you've got friends, neighbors, or coworkers who have babies. Ask the ones who nurse exclusively if you can have their free formula samples. They get all the same sample opportunities you do (at the hospital and pediatrician) but because they are breastfeeding, they don't need them.

Get Used to the Expense

While the options above will help you save money on formula, you'll still need to spend money and buy some. Formula will be critical to your twins' growth and development for the entire first year of their lives.

Once your babies are past the formula phase, you'll get to apply that money to your grocery budget to help feed your growing little ones.

FROM YOUR FELLOW FATHER OF TWINS... "Before the twins were born, I started to Google companies with twin discounts. I made a sizable list, wrote a form e-mail I could tweak depending on the ask, and started writing every company whose product I thought we might use. I couldn't believe the generosity of many companies out there. We had so many free samples, full size products, cases of formula, diapers, coupons with huge discounts, and so on. It took some time, but just in formula, we received over $500 in free products. That's a decent pay day, and I would have never had the time to do that after they were born!" - Jay Hahs

How Many Diapers Will You Need?

One of the big expenses with raising twins is diapers. From the day they are born until they master potty training and keeping their pants dry overnight, you'll need to buy diapers.

Twin Diaper Usage

Newborns average about 10 diapers a day per baby. So your newborn twins will need about 10 diapers × 30 days × 2 babies = at least 600 diapers for the first month.

After about a month, diaper consumption goes down to about 8 diapers per day. You'll need 8 diapers × 30 days × 2 babies = at least 480 diapers per month for a few more months.

After 3 to 6 months, your babies should fall into a regular pattern with more predictable diaper usage. The blowouts and leaks of the newborn days are gone and you'll see a pattern emerging. From 3 months to 1 year it should work down to about 4-6 diapers per day per child.

Based on averages (your twins' usage will vary) you are looking at using more than 2,000 diapers by the time your twins turn 6 months old.

After the 1 year mark, diaper use is usually down to about 4 a day: one change when they wake up, one before naps, one before bed, and one for the random poop that happens every day at unpredictable times. So your toddler twins will need 4 diapers × 30 days × 2 toddlers = 240 diapers per month.

Expect stacks of diapers in your home.

Your twins could use close to 3,000 diapers in the year between ages 1 and 2. From birth to age 2, your twins will use a grand total of over 7,000 diapers. (Makes you want to potty train early, doesn't it?)

You can also opt for cloth diapers. Cloth diapers will cost a couple hundred dollars to set up in the beginning. After that, it's a lot cheaper over time compared to disposable diapers.

Diaper Usage Over Time:

	1 mo.	2-3 mos.	3 mos. - 1 yr.	1-2 yrs.
Per Day Per Child	10	8	4 – 6	4
Total Per Month	600	480	240-360	240

Diaper Transition

Once your twins potty train, you'll be free from the traditional diapers. However, in some cases, you might need Pull-Ups for nap times and overnight sleeping until they master overnight dryness, too.

Unfortunately, Pull-Ups (and especially the overnight extra-absorbent kind) tend to be more expensive than regular diapers. Fortunately, the volume of diapers during this transition period is cut in half.

Diaper Budget

You will want to establish a generous diaper budget for yourself as you stock up on diapers during pregnancy and maintain regular diaper use through the first two years or so.

What should you do with that money after you don't need diapers? You'll see food consumption rise as your twins get older. That increased expense will likely offset any savings you see in no longer buying diapers.

Alternatively, you could start putting the money you would spend on diapers into your twins' college savings funds. That way when it is time for college, you can remind them that they don't have enough money because they refused to potty train until they were 4.

FROM YOUR FELLOW PARENT OF TWINS...
"At my baby shower we did a diaper raffle for a gift card to Target. For every pack of diapers you received a ticket. I am not lying to you when I say the boys are 5 months old now and I still have not had to buy one pack of diapers!" - Nicole Hafner

Paying for Medical Care

If you live in a country where you are responsible for your own medical expenses, then you must plan for the significant expense it will be just to get your twins here.

Prenatal Care

A twin pregnancy will result in more trips to the doctor than a singleton pregnancy. Perhaps you'll be visiting a specialist in multiple birth pregnancies. You'll get extra ultrasounds as the pregnancy progresses.

All of these doctor visits add up. Depending on how your health insurance is structured, you'll likely have out of pocket expenses all along the way.

Delivery Costs

Baby deliveries aren't cheap. When you combine two births at once, things get even more expensive. Add in twin delivery via C-section, which is more frequent with twin births, and the costs really start to climb. Expect at least $10,000 in delivery costs for a vaginal birth and more than $30,000 for a C-section. How much of that you pay will depend on your insurance.

Infant Care

After delivery, complications and baby care will multiply your medical expenses. If your babies spend any amount of time in the NICU, expect heavy expenses. On average, expect at least $3000 - $10,000 per day per child in the NICU. A family friend's twins spent nearly two months in the NICU. Expenses from their stay topped half a million dollars.

Later, you will have to pay for everything twice. You make one appointment for well-baby checkups, and everyone waits in the same room, but you pay for each child individually. You'll need to be ready for two bills.

Expecting Twins this Year?
Take Your Tax Deduction Now!

In the United States, the government is willing to financially help you with your twins. This comes in the form of a child tax credit and deductions for your dependents.

If you already have other children, you probably know about these benefits. If not, each child you have reduces your tax obligation to the government for the tax year. In my opinion, now is the time to reap these rewards for your soon-to-be-born twins, my friend. You need all the cash you can get.

If your twins are due this tax year, seriously consider adjusting your tax withholdings now so you can have the extra cash flow immediately.

We found out we were expecting twins in December. Our girls were due in the month of August. As soon as January rolled around that year, I gave my employer a new W-4 form that included the fact that I'd have four children total for that tax year.

Once your employer changes your tax withholdings, you'll be taking home more money. This is money that you'd get in the form of a tax return later had you not made the change. The bonus is that you get to use that money right now for baby-related purchases instead of giving it to Uncle Sam as an interest-free loan.

Update your tax deductions now so you don't say next year when you get your refund, "Oh, I really could have used this last year getting ready for the twins!"

Please note: I am not an accountant and my advice should be taken with a grain of salt. It worked for us but your situation may be different. When in doubt, talk to your accountant or lawyer.

Working After the Twins Arrive

You and your wife will want to discuss work arrangements for after the twins arrive. The right arrangement for your family will depend on several factors: lifestyle, child care, and work effectiveness.

Lifestyle

What do you want your family's lifestyle to be like after the twins are born? Do you want a parent to be home with the babies? Do you both have to work to pay the bills? Or do you both work to maintain a certain lifestyle?

What would you cut back on or sacrifice in your current lifestyle if you had only one income?

Child Care

How do you feel about others caring for and raising your children?

How much will child care cost you? Does the second spouse's income do more than cover that expense?

Can one parent take off at least a year or so to care for the twins?

Work Effectiveness

Even if you have child care during the day, you will still have to take care of the twins at night. During the first year, this nighttime care will cause a significant amount of sleep deprivation and wear you down. This will dramatically impact your effectiveness at work.

Consider the demands of both of your jobs to see how accommodating they are to any potential reduced performance. Is it realistic to have two sleep-deprived parents working below acceptable levels? If that is too risky, let one parent work and get decent sleep so they can keep the job and perform as needed to support the family.

Balance

You have to figure out what is most important to you. Lifestyle? Money? Raising your twins yourselves? Work?

Often, just the thought of twins causes dollar signs to flash before your eyes. Everyone knows that one baby isn't cheap; two seems exponentially more overwhelming. As parents, you both may feel that two incomes are needed just to provide for your new offspring. This may or may not be the case, depending on your priorities.

Twins require sacrifice of almost everything you currently take for granted, income included. However, the first year with twins is a blur and you can't assume that life will be just like it was before the twins were born.

As a couple, consider your situation from all angles before you make a united decision. Unity is ultimately what will make whatever you decide work.

FROM YOUR FELLOW FATHER OF TWINS...
"Given the cost of child care, I knew that something had to change for the eventual care of our children. My wife was cemented in her job as a teacher with great benefits and stability. I, on the other hand, was in a profession I didn't plan on being, and financially it had yet to be rewarding. After some quick math, I realized my net take-home pay after putting two children through child care at the same time would be nearly useless. It would be tough to go to work daily, 45-50 hours a week, knowing nearly all of my check was going towards someone else caring for our children.

My pregnant wife and I quickly agreed that I should become a stay-at-home dad. We were between a rock and a hard place financially. My going to work would have no real financial benefit, and the positives of raising our children at home quickly outweighed anything else. We would have to stop eating out, buying brand name everything, use consignment stores, and use the library and museum memberships to their fullest. It wouldn't be forever, but we felt that the sacrifices were worth it for me to be home with our children. 20 months later, I'm still at home, our quality of life has never been better. For 10+ years I was in a profession I didn't plan on, building my resume and waiting for that golden opportunity. I can now say I got it, and it's the most rewarding job I've ever had. All thanks to my twins." - Jay Hahs

Chapter Five

Gearing up for Twins

Minimalist Approach Will Save You Money

The manufacturers of baby products are very effective in creating specific tools for your babies.

If you are to financially survive twins, you don't need to buy a lot of these baby products. Oftentimes, you can get away with just buying one product and sharing it between your twins.

On one of our trips to the baby store, we saw a "tummy time mat" for sale. This product was colorfully decorated and had some built-in activities.

But you don't need a specialized mat for tummy time. Try a blanket on the floor. Problem solved.

Save the money. Think minimal. Ask yourself the following questions when considering new baby gear for your twins.

Do I Really Need This?

First, ask yourself: Can the main purpose of this piece of baby gear be handled manually or with something easily available around the house? What would I do if I didn't have this product?

Lots of baby gear is designed to do something that has been done with babies for centuries. Odds are you can get by with a low-tech or manual option to solve a particular problem. Think about how you can keep your babies warm, feed them, or change diapers without buying extra gear.

Seriously consider if you really can't live without the baby product you are considering. You can likely get by with a simpler (and cheaper) solution.

Will This Help With Twins?

Next, ask yourself: Do I need this piece (or two) of baby gear to be able to handle and care for both babies at the same time?

Caring for twins becomes extremely demanding when there is only one caregiver. If you'll be home alone with the twins, it is OK to have some baby gear that will help ease your ability to care for them.

For example, we had two bouncy seats so we could lay each of our infant girls in them for feeding. This made it extremely easy for one person to simultaneously bottle feed our twins.

Having Twins Doesn't Mean You Need Two of Everything

What are some items that you can get away with having only one of instead of two?

If you already have a child or two, or even if twins are your induction to parenthood, try to think about possible scenarios where your twins can take turns using one piece of baby gear. For example, you need only:

- One baby bath, but two towels
- One changing table, but diaper supplies for two
- One playpen or play set where you can sit one baby on each side
- One bedroom that the twins can share
- One of any given toy until the twins are old enough to both want the same toy at the same time
- One wardrobe of clothes, particularly if you have identical twins that can share everything they wear

Be judicious with your purchases. You'll need double of a lot of things with twins, but there is no need to spend more money than is necessary. Your twins will share a lot as they grow up together. You might as well start them early.

Shopping Online for Twin Products

As a parent of twins, you'll likely want to purchase twin related products like books, clothes, gifts, etc. for both your twins and yourself.

Here's a list of several online stores that offer products specifically for twins and parents of twins:

- Just Multiples: justmultiples.com
- Trends In Twos: trendsintwos.com
- Twin T-Shirt Company: twintshirtcompany.com
- Twin Z Pillow: twinznursingpillow.com

Can Twins Sleep in the Same Crib?

The current recommendation by the American Academy of Pediatrics is that each twin should sleep in his or her own crib.

There should be nothing at all in the crib, except for one baby, and what that one baby is wearing. To reduce the risk of Sudden Infant Death Syndrome make sure that there are no blankets, stuffed animals, or bumper pads in the crib. The crib mattress sheet needs to fit tightly and be snug.

If you still choose to have both twins in the same crib, here is how that worked with our twins:

At the hospital, the nurses had our twins together in the same bassinet. When we got home, we just continued this pattern. From their time in utero, each twin had constantly been with their sibling. Why not continue?

We found that our babies would actually turn toward each other when they were sleeping side by side in the same crib. As newborns, your babies aren't going to move around much, so where you put them is where they will stay.

What about Noisy, Wiggly Babies?

Eventually your babies will start to wiggle and hit each other. Don't freak out. They were doing this in the womb for months (just ask your wife). If it doesn't bother them, it shouldn't bother you.

Our twins slept in the same crib until they were big enough to bother each other during the night.

So you may ask: Don't they wake each other up if they sleep in the same room or crib? No, not necessarily. Typically one twin can sleep through the cries of the other. You'll even find one of your babies with arms or legs sprawled over the other, and both twins are sleeping contently.

When to Separate

We kept our girls in the same crib for several months until they started getting bigger and rolling around. We knew it was time to separate them when, one night, we were jarred from sleep because Twin A had put her foot in Twin B's head and Twin B was crying.

When that time arrived, we put two cribs in the same room, with one baby in each. The girls seemed to miss each other at first but would call out to each other via squawks or gurgles in a form of echolocation (think bats) to make sure their sister was near.

Another option is a crib made specifically for twins. It has two beds, but they are joined in some way, some even like a bunk bed. These can be very expensive or have mattresses that are not the standard size, but it may help you save some space. Pamco and Duetta both make such twin cribs.

Crib Positions

We liked to have our cribs close enough to each other that one parent could stand between them and still reach in and soothe two crying babies in two different cribs.

As our twins got older and were more able to distract each other, we moved the cribs to opposite ends of the bedroom. This helped minimize their interactions with each other when it came time for naps and bedtime since they tended to play, talk to each other, and distract each other from falling asleep.

Two Beds

When the time comes to move out of the cribs, you'll probably want two beds, too. You should be able to fit two twin-sized beds (yes, they call them twin beds) in the floor space of even a small bedroom. Alternatively, you can look at bunk beds or a trundle bed to economize space.

Advantages of Sharing a Room

- You only have to decorate one room.
- When you hear one of your twins crying in the middle of the night, you don't have to figure out which bedroom to run to.
- All the kids' clothes will be in one room, which makes it easy for dressing when they are young and makes it easy to share clothes (especially if you have identical twins).
- If you put both your twins in the same room, you don't have to buy a bigger house right away.

Disadvantages of Sharing a Room

- As they get older, your twins will wake each other up. Most often this happens in the morning, when you are hoping for a few more minutes of sleep.
- Quieting down for bedtime is a challenge. Our girls liked to chatter and sing to each other after we put them in their cribs. This led to about an hour of activity before they calmed down and finally went to sleep.
- Naps in the same room are difficult because your twins will just want to play with each other and not sleep.

- Boy/girl twins will eventually reach the age where sharing a room is awkward.

Changing Table for Twins

For the first year or so of their lives, your twins will go through a lot of diapers. Having a good changing table can make those frequent diaper changes easier on you and your back. Also, it is nice to have your wipes, diapers, hand sanitizer and other changing supplies all in one place so you don't have to go looking for them when you discover a twin with a messy diaper.

One changing table should be enough for your twins. They likely will not always need changes at the same times, and if they do, one can wait a minute.

Dedicated changing tables can be relatively inexpensive. Some are just a series of shelves with a pad on the top shelf where you can rest your baby. The shelves are important because you'll want to store all the supplies for changing your twins.

You can set up a changing table on almost any flat surface, so you don't have to think of a changing table as a unique item of furniture in your nursery. Several dressers are made with a changing area on top. If your dresser is the right height, you could buy a cushion to put on the top to make a changing table. Another idea is a changing table that hangs on the rails of a crib. It stores out of the way when the child is sleeping.

While the changing table was great for changing babies, I figure that at least half the time or more we changed diapers somewhere else. Typically the family room floor doubled as the unofficial changing table. Don't spend too much money on a changing table for your twins because an existing dresser or floor can do the job if needed.

Twin Car Seats

You'll need two car seats, one for each twin. Don't skimp or buy a used seat with an unknown history. Your twins need to be safe and comfortable.

You'll need a car seat for each twin.

While our twins were infants, we used two Graco Infant Car Seats simply because we already had them. These were good for carrying the baby into the store, church, or house while they were sleeping and not having to wake them up to move them.

However, they quickly grew out of these car seats and we needed to upgrade. We purchased two Britax Roundabout Convertible Car Seats that performed very well. You can put your twins in them rear facing and then transition them to front facing after they turn 1. Depending on how big your twins get and what version of car seat you purchase, the Britax should last you until they weigh at least 50 pounds (23 kg), well into toddlerhood.

Air Travel

To make air travel easier, we were motivated to buy the Britax because it was more compact and considerably lighter than other available models. Imagine one parent carrying two car seats and carry-on bags through the airport while the other parent wrangles the twins. You'll want lightweight seats!

Cleaning

Also consider how easy the straps are to remove. Yes, the straps. Not just the cover. Your twins will, at some point, vomit or have an accident while in their car seat, and removal of both the seat cover and straps will be important in the cleaning process.

Twin Strollers

*An inline double baby stroller is one of the
best things you can get for your twins.*

Transporting your twins is a challenge worthy of being
included on "The Amazing Race." You're leaving the house
with twins? You're awesome. Pat yourself on the back.

However, gone are the days of up and deciding to go somewhere on the fly. Now you find yourself getting the babies

(and anyone else) ready to leave at least 30 minutes before you actually need to leave the house.

There's a lot to think about and a lot to remember to make sure outings go smoothly once you leave the safety of your home. So do yourself a favor and get an inline double baby stroller.

We bought a Baby Trend Double Snap N Go Stroller Frame that easily fit both our Graco car seat/infant carriers. I can safely say that this piece of baby gear is unequivocally the best purchase we made for our infant twins.

The Snap N Go is light, compact, easy to maneuver, and you never have to disturb a sleeping baby by taking him out of the car seat. Just lift the car seats out of the car, snap them into the stroller base, and go. Once you are done with your inline stroller, you can easily resell it on Craigslist or at a garage sale. Snap N Go strollers are very popular and in high demand.

Inline vs. Side-by-Side

There are a bazillion stroller options out there. Thankfully, having twins narrows that number to a couple hundred. But really, there are only two basic types: inline and side-by-side.

You'll have to weigh the pros and cons of each kind based on your situation and the way you think you'll use a stroller. The reality is that you may end up trying both kinds over the course of infancy and early childhood, and that different types of strollers will work for you at different stages of life.

Side-by-side strollers work great once your twins can sit up.

How Long Will It Last?

In our case, we started with the inline stroller and then moved to a side-by-side. The inline stroller lasted until our girls got long enough to kick the other car seat, and consequently, her sister's head. (We hit this problem about the 6-month mark.)

Once our twins could sit up on their own, we switched to a more basic double side-by-side stroller. Because these umbrella-type strollers don't need the bulky car seat carriers, they take up less space and aren't such a wide load problem. We found ours to be pretty rugged and able to handle everything from airports to dirt paths at the park. It was definitely sturdy enough to take whatever our twins could throw at it.

FROM YOUR FELLOW TWIN PARENT...
"I'm grateful that we spent the money on a tandem stroller that accommodated car seats. There was nothing better than taking the twins out for a stroll in the neighborhood only to have them fall asleep in their car seats and stay there sleeping for two-plus hours. Blissful time to rest, take a shower, or have quality time with other loved ones." - Diane Rau

Twin Diaper Bag

You don't need two diaper bags for twins. You just need a diaper bag that is designed to hold enough items to accommodate twin babies. The Skip Hop Duo Double Deluxe Diaper Bag is praised by many parents as the best diaper bag for twins. It is spacious and will fit all the diapers, bottles, extra clothes and formula you need.

Twin Feeding Pillows

When feeding your twins, it is helpful to have a twin feeding pillow. These pillows help support the twins on your lap in a position where it is easy to feed them. They are especially helpful for breastfeeding mothers so that Mom doesn't have to hold the twins during the entire feeding. But beyond meal time, these twin feeding pillows can also help during playtime or nap time.

One important feature is a removable cover. When your twins spit up on the feeding pillow, you can simply throw the cover in the wash rather than having to treat the entire pillow. It may even be handy to buy a second cover for your pillow so you don't have to wait while one is in the wash.

Other features to look for are a carrying strap, a privacy sheet (for nursing mothers) and whether the feeding pillow can have more than one use. Some can be used as a back rest or to help the twins learn to sit up.

FROM YOUR FELLOW PARENT OF TWINS...
"I am glad that we got the My Brest Friend twin pillow. This helped us last as long as we did breastfeeding." - Jessica Gibbons

High Chairs and Booster Seats

You don't need high chairs for your infant twins unless you have the money to spend and lots of square footage in the kitchen. High chairs are generally expensive and take up a lot of space. Most people typically buy booster seats as a transition piece between the high chair and sitting at the table unassisted.

Instead, get only booster seats and you'll be able to use them a lot longer and save some money in the process.

Booster seats are cheaper and more portable
than high chairs, so they're great for twins.

We used two Fisher-Price Booster Seats for our twin girls and loved them. They are simple to clean and are portable so you can easily take them to Grandma's house.

Picking Practical Baby Clothes

As a dad, you may not care what clothing style or designs your twins wear. However, there is one thing that will directly impact your happiness as a dad: snaps.

You see, baby clothes usually have easy access for diaper changes. If you are looking at baby clothes that don't have snaps on the bottom to make a diaper change easy, walk away and buy something else.

If you have both boys and girls, you'll notice that girls' clothes are usually more ornate and tend to have more pieces that need to be buttoned or snapped together.

Unfortunately for dads of girls, this means that you will be trying to get your daughters dressed in clothes that were designed for looks and not for ease-of-use.

Buttons on baby clothes are your worst enemy. You'll be trying to dress a wiggly baby and can't get the buttons buttoned. Or you'll be changing a diaper in the middle of the night and can't get the buttons undone.

The lesson: avoid buttons at all costs. Sure, buttons make outfits "cute" and "precious," but you don't care. Buttons on a baby outfit turn even a steady-handed surgeon into a fumble-fingered failure.

So when you go shopping for your kids, or your wife brings home a stack of new baby clothes, be sure you ask the only question that really matters: "These have snaps, right?"

When to Make Preparations

We started getting ready for our twins as soon as we found out that we were expecting them.

You've got a small window of opportunity between when you discover you're having twins and that tough third trimester. During the first trimester, mom typically has morning sickness that may last all day. So she may not be able to help much at first. During the middle part of the pregnancy, there's a sweet spot when mom feels good and you can get your preparations done. The third trimester is when you get into the risk of bed rest and early arrival of your twins.

Try to get as much done as you can before the 30-week mark. Then you can just put the finishing touches on preparations and get ready for your twins' arrival.

Perhaps you haven't found out the sexes of your twins yet. If you want to begin preparations right away and you're early in the pregnancy, you can always go for non-gender specific items for your twins like cribs, stroller, car seats, bottles, diapers, etc. After you learn what you're having, you can prepare nursery decorations and gender specific clothing.

Always Ask for the Twin Discount

As you prepare for your twins and stock up on the necessary twin baby gear, you will be spending lots of money. Make sure you don't spend more than you need to. You need to find discounts.

Remember: it never hurts to ask. Larger stores sometimes offer discounts, so just ask. For example, we bought our car seats for the twins from Babies R Us. They gave us a "twin discount" of 10 percent off because we bought two of the same thing.

If you are shopping at a smaller, local business, you may have even better luck because you're more likely to garner sympathy from the more attentive business owner or store employee.

Get into the mindset when buying baby gear for your twins: "How can I get a discount on this?"

FROM YOUR FELLOW FATHER OF TWINS... "The best thing we did prior to the birth of our girls was get as much support as possible. My wife joined a Twin Mom club while she was still pregnant and they were willing to pass down second hand clothing, extra diapers, and even sell us equipment at a very large discount.

My favorite product was the Baby Trend Snap-N-Go Stroller. I loved that stroller. We purchased it second hand and then passed it on to another expectant family later.

The best realization was that we do not have to have everything new. Look at second hand and don't be fearful to ask for help!" - Tyler Williamson

More Gear Recommendations

For up to date gear recommendations for your twins, visit dadsguidetotwins.com/extras

Chapter Six

Preparing for Delivery

Visit the Hospital

Your twins' arrival shouldn't be the first time you see the hospital and its facilities.

Take a tour of where you want your twins to be delivered and make sure you have answers to questions about what happens on delivery day. What level of care can their neonatal intensive care unit provide premature babies?

Ask your doctor about hospitals in your city that your twins may be sent to and under what circumstances they would be transferred to those locations.

You need to consider where you'll be delivering your twins. Is it close to home? Is it close to work? Is it close to family?

Think about how you're going to travel back and forth. If your twins do end up in the NICU, you'll be visiting them multiple times a day.

What to Pack for the Hospital

What should you, the dad, take to the hospital?

Make sure your wife has everything she needs to be comfortable and that you've got clothes and car seats for the twins.

You'll most likely be spending a few nights (at least) at the hospital after the twins are born.

You need to make sure you have food to sustain yourself. Pack trail mix and other quick snacks that you can grab when you have a free moment. You can even make arrangements for friends to bring in some meals for you. Your wife will get food from the hospital, but you will most likely be relegated to the cafeteria, which will get old really fast.

You'll need sleeping supplies. You do not want to sleep on the hospital room couch without any extra padding. Just plan like you are going camping: take a pillow, sleeping bag, and a personal mattress (foam or self inflating) that you can put down on the couch or floor if needed.

Make sure you've got your laptop or smartphone (with charger) to upload pictures and share the news with your friends and family.

Prepare to Capture the Moment

As a proud father, you'll want to document the arrival of your twins for future posterity.

To do so, you need to be prepared with a plan for getting the pictures and video you want.

You need to keep in mind how your twins will arrive, where they will arrive, and what you will be doing during delivery.

How the Twins Arrive

Your twins will arrive in one of two ways: naturally down the path God created or a more direct route courtesy of a Cesarean section procedure. Either way they arrive, they will come one at a time.

Where the Twins will Arrive

Where you are when the twins are delivered often depends on how they are being delivered. You may be in a birthing room for a natural delivery or in an operating room for a C-section.

The "where" may restrict when you can take pictures or video. Be sure to ask your doctor when discussing delivery options early in the pregnancy if you can take pictures and video of the delivery.

Some doctors will be video shy. If you have a good rapport with your doctor, take some time to discuss their concerns, your desires, and find out exactly what the hospital policy is.

If it's important enough to you and your doc is adamantly against video and pictures, then you may need to find a new care provider.

Right Equipment

For the birth of our twins, I used a digital camera that also takes video. To the outside observer, it looks like a camera, which your medical staff shouldn't mind.

The sneaky part was that I could switch to video mode and capture my girls' first moments while the medical staff thought I was taking pictures. (We hadn't gotten a clear yes or no from our doctor about her video preferences.)

If you walk into the operating room, for example, with big and obvious video-recording equipment, they may not let you use it.

You can always use your smartphone to take pictures and video of the birth. However, if you want higher quality images, consider using a dedicated digital camera.

Timing

Time starts to speed up once the first baby is emerging from mommy. You need to be Johnny-on-the-spot and have that camera ready. If you have a digital camera or phone that takes video, you can switch modes and keep rolling.

Once your first twin is born, you'll likely follow her over to the warming bed where the nurses suck out her nose and mouth, get her cleaned up, and swaddle her in some blankets.

You'll be so excited that you may forget there is another one coming. Keep an eye and ear on what is happening with the second delivery so you can quickly move back to your wife and have the camera ready for your next child.

I struggled with wanting to see my firstborn twin, comfort my wife, and watch the second birth all at the same time. Nevertheless, I managed to get video of both births and of their first few moments of life.

Awesome Experience

Watching your twins be delivered is an amazing experience that you will never forget. Plan to be there and be prepared to capture the moment for the future. After all, your wife won't be taking pictures during delivery, so it is up to you.

When taking photos of your twins, you'll want to remember that twins are individuals. Of course you may want a picture of the two of them, but consider taking individual photos as well. This will help them develop their own identity.

What does it mean when your twins are breech?

Breech in any pregnancy means that the baby is positioned with their butt or feet (instead of the head) closer to the exit of the vaginal canal.

Ideally, both babies will be head down. That gives you the option to have a natural vaginal delivery of your twins. Many doctors won't even try a vaginal birth, if one or both of the twins is breech.

Your babies can be in many different positions while they are in the womb. You'll know as you approach delivery how the twins are positioned because of the frequent ultrasounds.

Talk to your physician about options for getting babies in the position that you would like, and if that's not possible, what that means for the delivery. Does it mean a definite C-section or is vaginal birth still an option?

When your babies are breech, it's not the end of the world. They should still be born very healthy and happy. They just may not be born the way that you are hoping. For example, if you are hoping for a vaginal birth, you may instead have to get a C-section for your babies.

W H A T   M O M   E X P E R I E N C E D . . .
"I really thought I'd be able to deliver them naturally. I just convinced myself that I'd be able to get it done, and not have to do a C-section. When one of the babies was breech, I thought I'd be able to get her to turn, so I could have a natural delivery. I couldn't get her to turn, and then her brother stopped growing, so we had to do surgery because she was still breech. Ugh!" - Grace Nakamoto

What Your Wife Feels During a Twin C-Section

My wife has ended up having a C-section with all three of our deliveries (four kids). Twins are more likely than not to come via C-section, so it is in your best interest to be ready.

As a dad, you will experience a C-section from the outside. Nevertheless, you need to be there to support, encourage, and help. I asked my wife to share her side of the story so that you, as a dad, can know what to expect and what your wife will be going through before, during, and after a C-section.

I've put "dad's view" comments mixed in with my wife's story to also give you some perspective of what I saw and experienced as the dad of twins delivered via C-section. In my wife's own words...

C-Section Preparations

If you are brave enough to venture down the "What if" of the C-section path, a good place to start is to ask your doctor about the specifics of what to expect, because procedures undoubtedly vary from hospital to hospital and even doctor to doctor within the same hospital. Some of what I experienced may hold true across the board; some may not. I share my experience to help you get a sense of what to expect.

After filling out a lot of paperwork and signing an awful

lot of papers, Joe and I walked down to the Operating Room. I kissed Joe and followed the nurse into the room, leaving him in the hall to wait. My nurse helped me up onto the operating table so I was sitting on it.

The anesthesiologist numbed the skin on my back prior to administering a spinal block, so it just felt like a little pinch. I didn't feel the needle going in. The spinal takes effect immediately. I had time to swing my legs up onto the operating table before they started to go numb, and within minutes I was numb from my toes to my ribs. My body felt heavy and warm and it was kind of funny to try to move and not have anything happen. I could feel some pressure, like when you take your hand and press it on your arm, when the nurses were disinfecting my stomach to prep for surgery.

Dad's View – I missed all of this. I was outside the operating room, dressed up in a "bunny suit" (covering my clothes and hair) waiting for the nurse to come get me and let me in. Time passed very slowly and about the time I started to think they forgot me, the nurse came out and ushered me into the operating room.

What Mom Sees During Delivery

When they were actually ready to get going, they let Joe come into the OR. They put a curtain up at my chest so I couldn't see anything that was going on. It was wide enough and high enough that Joe could just see over it standing. After our first C-section, I realized I hated not being able to see anything, so with the second and third ones, I made sure to request that they lower the curtain when the babies were coming out. This enabled me to see each twin as they lifted her from my belly, but I couldn't see my belly.

Dad's View – By the time I was ushered into the room, the medical staff was already busy at work cutting open my wife. Our doctor actually wanted me to sit down (and thus not see anything) until closer to the actual delivery. I spent this time talking to my wife in a surreal setting where everything was covered up except her head. Her arms were stretched out to the sides and the anesthesiologist was there with us. The whole time, I hoped the doctor would let me stand up in time to see the delivery.

What Mom Feels During Delivery

You really won't feel any of it. You may feel some pressure and you may sense your body being rocked back and forth as they ease the babies out, but other than that, nothing. Since you won't feel anything, you may want to ask your doctor or your husband to narrate the events for you so you know where you are in the process and what is going on. Otherwise, you just get to lie there, wait, and wonder, and the whole experience will be over before you know it.

Dad's View – As I stood up next to my wife and peered over the curtain, I narrated what was happening to my wife while balancing the camera and trying to remember to take pictures and video. I'm not sure how much I actually said to my wife but I did get the video!

Reliving the Moment

Joe was able to video the births, and I actually love watching that footage. It's not gross–very cool, actually. I thought that I would be cut open from hip to hip and they would just lift the babies out, but the incision is only big enough for the baby's head to pass through. I remember being amazed at how much of a "mini birth canal" experience it still was.

Dad's View – Watching the doctor pull our babies out of my wife was amazing. I was surprised how much the doctor had to pull, push, yank, and twist to get one of our daughters out.

Baby's First Moments

After the babies were out (about two minutes apart), they took them over to the warmer to wipe them down and do their APGAR test (to determine how well the babies tolerated the birthing process). Once they got them bundled up, they brought them over for me to see. I could touch them with one hand and kiss their little cheeks when the nurses held them close to my face.

Unfortunately, at this point, you're not really in a position where you can hold your babies. Then it was off to the nursery for them.

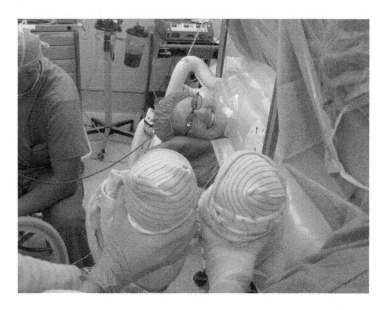

If the twins are born by C-section, Mom won't really be in a position to hold them until later.

Dad's View – I was mentally torn between watching my first-born daughter get cleaned up and then rushing back to the operating table to see my other daughter be born. I also wanted to tell my wife how our first girl was doing. My head was swirling but I somehow managed to see the first, tell my wife, and not miss the second's birth.

Sewing Mommy Back Up

At this point I encouraged Joe to go with the babies. He really didn't need to be around for me to get stitched up, and by going with the babies, he could keep taking pictures and video that I could look at later instead of both of us missing those first minutes.

Back in the OR, it took another 10-15 minutes for them to stitch me up. (It's a lot of lying there just looking at the ceiling while you process a lot of emotion! But hang in there. You'll see your babies again soon!) I asked the doctor ahead of time if they would show me the placenta before they threw it away. That was cool for me. The placenta was a lot bigger than I imagined and it was cool to see those two little umbilical cords coming out of it.

Dad's View – Since I went out of the operating room with our girls I missed all of this. The next time I saw my wife she was wheeled into recovery and covered in a mountain of blankets.

Right After C-Section

After getting stitched up, I was wheeled to recovery for observation for about an hour. Then it was back to my room and I was able to get acquainted with my babies. After probably another hour, the feeling started coming back to my legs and I could wiggle my toes again. I had an IV and a catheter for the first 24 hours post-surgery.

Moving Around

I received some good advice from my nurse after my second son's C-section. She told me my recovery would be quickest if I started moving around as soon as I could. I vaguely remembered being encouraged to move with my first surgery, and I didn't. I just lay in bed unless I had to go to the bathroom. As a result, it took me nearly a month before I could walk like a normal person again without being all hunched over. So I took the advice with No. 2 and even though I was hooked up to the IV and catheter, I would try to stand up with help every hour or two and take a few steps around my bed.

As soon as the catheter was out, I would walk around the room (with assistance for the first day) and to the bathroom, and by Day 2 or 3, I was moving like a pro. So if you go the C-section route, it pays to move as much and as often as you can. I also did this with the twins and had a great recovery with them.

Dad's View – Because surgery patients are at a high risk of falling, I made sure to be near so I could help my wife move around or go to the bathroom. This also helped her get in and out of bed more easily than if she had been alone.

Drug Side Effects

Some of the side effects of the drugs that go along with the spinal (that I experienced, anyway) are shaking, nausea, and itching. Once the delivery was over, they were able to give me something to help stop the shaking and the nausea. But I had intense itching for 24-48 hours after delivery that I just had to wait out until the meds were out of my system.

With the shaking, it was more like extreme shivering. Granted, the OR was cold, so I wasn't sure how much of the shaking was due to that, or if I was more nervous than I realized and the shaking was due to nerves. But when it still hadn't stopped after delivery, I asked about it and they were able to give me something that stopped it pretty quickly.

Dad's View – It was disturbing to see my wife shaking violently right after a major surgery. Fortunately, the medical staff got that under control quickly. The initial recovery room is where I really got to see my girls, study them for the first time (the operating room was so rushed), and help them meet their mom.

Recovery and Pain Management

Other than having to hold a pillow on my stomach to brace it if I needed to cough, sneeze, or laugh for the first few days, it was not a bad recovery considering a C-section is a major surgery.

Try to stay ahead of your pain, as that will aid in your recovery. If you start to hurt, you've waited too long to ask for meds. And it may seem unlikely, but by the time your prescription for Percocet has been used up, you will be able to manage your pain with ibuprofen. I know it's hard to compare to other women, but I think that even with a C-section, I have had an easier recovery than some friends who tore during a vaginal delivery and also had to have stitches.

Dad's View – When my wife stayed ahead of the pain by taking the pain pills slightly ahead of schedule, everything went pretty smoothly. One of our first nights in the hospital post twin C-section, our nurse was giving my wife a lower than expected dosage because we apparently didn't ask for more. My wife was in quite a bit of pain and very miserable. So don't be afraid to ask! If your wife can't, you need to do it for her. I kept a log of when she needed to take her medicine and that helped keep us on track even when we were sleep deprived.

Incision

You will be bandaged from hip to hip, and when they take the bandage off, it will look like you were cut from hip to hip, too. But you really weren't. Imagine blowing up a balloon and drawing a smiley face on it. When you deflate it, the smile gets a lot smaller. Same principle with your belly. By the time your body bounces back from the pregnancy, you will have about a 4-inch-long scar right along your lower abdomen.

Bottom Line

I made it to 36 weeks and 3 days with our twin girls. We felt very lucky and very blessed that our girls were healthy and didn't run into any problems. But there are lots of twin parents out there who have the NICU as some part of their hospital experience. Your twin delivery may very well be different from ours.

So bottom line here? Make sure you move around (sitting, standing, walking) as soon as you can after surgery and after that, as much as you can. Ask your doctor for clarification on the details if you really feel like you need to know play-by-play what is going to happen, because it may not happen for you exactly like it did for me.

Is a Natural Birth of Twins Possible?

The most important factor in determining if you can have a natural, vaginal delivery of twins is how the babies are positioned inside Mom prior to birth.

Just like singleton babies, the twin closest to the cervix will need to be head down to be born naturally. If your baby is breech (feet or rump down) or transverse (laying sideways), your C-section is all but certain unless the baby can be maneuvered into the right position.

Even if you are attempting a natural birth of twins, your doctor and medical staff will monitor your babies very closely during labor. Mom will also likely be prepared for surgery just in case there are complications and an emergency C-section is required.

Occasionally, Baby A will be born vaginally but Baby B gets stressed or is stuck and has to be delivered via C-section. This is often called a "double whammy" because Mom has to go through the physical, mental, and emotional challenges of both a natural birth followed by the major abdominal surgery of a C-section.

If all goes smoothly with the natural delivery, expect Baby B to arrive anywhere from a few minutes to half an hour or more after the first twin.

Preparation During the Pregnancy

You should discuss your wishes with your doctor so all arrangements can be made and expectations properly set. Even if you want to have a natural birth of twins, please learn about twin C-sections so you can be prepared if that is how your babies need to be delivered.

If all other plans fall apart, the safe and healthy delivery of your babies is your ultimate goal. Keep that perspective as you're planning for your twins' arrival.

Preemies and the NICU

Your twin pregnancy has a higher chance of resulting in premature babies than a regular singleton pregnancy. Accepting that your twins may have to spend time in the Neonatal Intensive Care Unit may help you prepare for that situation. You may want to arrange for a tour of your closest NICU before your wife delivers.

What happens when your babies arrive early? Don't expect to see your babies right after delivery. They will be whisked away to be checked and stabilized before you get to see them.

Shortly thereafter, your little ones will be covered in wires and tubes that seem to be disproportionately large compared to their tiny bodies. These tubes and wires will be connected to monitoring machines and an oxygen supply.

The machines will have alert monitors set up that sound an alarm if critical levels are reached (for example, heart rate, breathing, blood oxygen level).

You may not be able to hold your babies for weeks. When you do see and hold your babies, focus on the positive and good in the situation. Eventually you may be able to even take your older kids with you to the hospital. Oftentimes there are viewing windows where the kids or family members can look through the window into the nursery and see the babies without actually going into the NICU.

This will help your other kids understand why their baby sister or brother has not come home yet. Visits to the hospital help siblings see the twins and start to get used to them before they even come home.

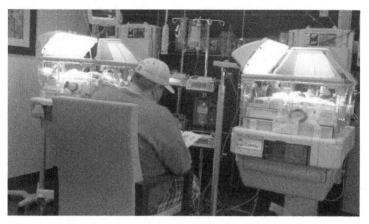

It is common for twins to spend some time in the NICU. But you can still be a dad while they're there.

Take joy in the upcoming milestones as your babies move off the ventilators, can wear clothes, and pass the car seat test to go home.

One of your babies may come home before the other. You'll get used to a new schedule and baby in the home and then it will change when the other comes home. Finally, with both babies at home, you can settle into the routine of having your compete family all in one place.

FROM YOUR FELLOW FATHER OF TWINS...
"Surviving the NICU and working through the struggles of having them born at 24 weeks was definitely the biggest surprise and struggle we have had. We asked a lot of questions to make sure we were educated on what was happening and what we could expect. We also dove in to take care of changing diapers, taking temperatures, and handling feedings. Just being there with our girls was so important and I truly believe it aided in their ability to make the strides they did and make it home before their due date." - Matthew Gray

Chapter Seven

Decide Now

How to Name Your Twins

Naming any baby can be a challenge. After all, you and the child will have to live with that name for many years to come.

Many of the same questions that come up with naming a single baby are applicable to naming twins:

- Does this name remind me of someone else I liked or disliked?
- What are the nicknames for this name?
- What do the initials for this name spell? Anything we'd regret?
- Do we want to honor a family member by using that name?
- How easy is the name to spell and say? Will the twins constantly be correcting people their entire lives?

Twins may arrive on the same day and may look the same, but each twin is an individual person.

So remember your twins' individuality when deciding on what names to give them.

You may be tempted to give your twins rhyming names. Although this may sound cute, don't do it. Your twins will have to live with their names their entire lives.

Put any potential twin name to the test:

- Will your twin baby's name still sound good, professional, and practical when she heads off to college?
- How about on a resume for a job?
- As a byline in a news article?
- On that Nobel Prize she will win?

Cut the overt cuteness and give your twins a name that will still sound good long after they outgrow their newborn diapers.

Using a Theme for Twin Names

You may want to have twin baby names that fit a theme. Themes can be subtle based on religion, places, or cultural heritage. Perhaps you could even give each child a name with a similar meaning.

Twin Naming No-Nos

Please, at all costs, avoid naming your kids some stereotypical twin name pairs like Luke and Leia or Bonnie and Clyde. Hey, I love Star Wars as much as the next guy, but I'm not putting that burden on my twin babies.

Twin Names that Mean "Twin"

You can be clever and name your twins a name that actually means "twin" in a foreign or ancient language. That can be your private inside joke as most people will never know.

Naming Same Gender Twins

Every ultrasound you get during the pregnancy will identify your twins as Baby A and Baby B. One thing you could do is name your babies alphabetically based on these labels.

Baby A gets the first name alphabetically, and Baby B gets the second name alphabetically. For example, if you are having twin girls and you wanted to name them Amy and Elaine, Baby A could be Amy and Baby B could be Elaine.

You can also wait until you meet the twins and observe their personalities and their appearance and then match the name that best fits the baby at that time.

However you decide to name your twins, it's good to have several names up front before your twins are born. You can even decide before they're born which baby will be which name.

Final Twin Name Check

Go to your back door, open the door, and yell into the backyard your two twin names in rapid succession as if you were calling them for dinner.

Do they sound good? Will your neighbors think you're crazy when they hear those names over the coming years? If your names pass this final test, you're good to go.

How to Tell Your Twins Apart

One of the big challenges that any twin dad faces is telling his twins apart.

Even non-identical, or fraternal, twins may look very similar upon arrival.

You need a system in place to know how you will identify each baby. This is important for your sanity, tracking who needs to eat, and being able to identify which kid is in the baby pictures ten years from now.

There are several schools of thought on identifying twins. We opted for one that would be obvious at a distance and in pictures: color coding. We dressed one girl in warm colors (pinks, reds, yellows) and the other in cool colors (blues, greens, purples).

Color coding works best once you get them home from the hospital. If you are worried, keep their hospital name bands on until you are ready.

For those initial pictures at the hospital where the babies are all swaddled up in identical blankets and head warmers, you need a context clue as to who is who. I put a little piece of yellow paper in the background of pictures that I took of our oldest daughter. That way when I looked at the pictures later, I knew which newborn was which.

Should Twins Sleep in the Parent's Room?

You may consider having your infant twins sleep in your room for several months. Twin parents will often put a bassinet or Pack-n-Play in their room where the twins can sleep.

The American Academy of Pediatrics recommends that parents have their babies sleep in the same room with them for at least six months and ideally the entire first year.

There are advantages of sleeping twins in your room:

- Easy to access – When your twins are in your room, you don't have to go far to take care of them. This is great during middle-of-the-night, sleep-deprived feeding sessions.

- Easy to monitor – Because your twins are in the same room, you can easily listen and monitor them. You don't need an electronic baby monitor and can easily roll over and see the babies to confirm if you really need to get out of bed.

There are also some disadvantages to this arrangement:

- Impacts your sleep – You will hear every sound your twins make when they sleep in your room. Even benign noises will rouse you from your sleep.

- Harder to transition later – Even at an early age, your twins will get used to the patterns you are setting. Eventually they will have to move to their own room. Depending on your kids, this transition may be difficult.

- No space for you – I like to think of my bedroom as my sanctuary. With twins, your house will be a mess, and you need some place that is reserved for you to rest and relax.

We put our twin girls in their own room from the first night we were home from the hospital. Fortunately, their room was right next door to ours. This made monitoring and access a lot easier than if our house floor plan had put greater distance between us.

Having the girls sleep in their own room made it easier for us to rest when we did sleep and got them used to sleeping on their own.

Should You Breastfeed or Bottle Feed Twins?

There always seems to be a lively debate about whether you should breastfeed or bottle feed babies. The advances in formula have made the health questions behind that decision pretty close to call. Yes, breast milk is ultimately the best, but you shouldn't feel bad if you decide to go the formula route.

As a father of twins, what to feed your babies is more of a logistical question: how will you physically be able to feed two babies at the same time?

Benefits of Breastfeeding

With our first two kids, my wife breastfed and we were happy with that decision. I think dads should be big fans of breastfeeding. Why?

- You don't have to do anything. Unless your wife pumps milk to be served later, you aren't going to be feeding any babies.

- You don't have to buy baby formula, and thus you save tons of cash.

- You don't have to wash out bottles and related supplies all the time.

All this sounds great when you have a single baby. But what about twins?

Sorry guys, twins are a game changer. As much as you'd love to reap the benefits described previously, the decision on whether to breastfeed or bottle feed twins is simple: Do whatever your wife wants. Why? Logistics.

Breastfeeding Option

Breastfeeding twins is not a simple feat. How do you feed them at the same time? Getting one baby positioned properly and latched on so she can feed is a two-hand job. Until breastfeeding is established and both Mom and the babies feel like they have it, Mom is going to need some help getting both babies latched on.

I recommend that your wife talk to a few other Mothers of Multiples (MoMs) who have successfully breastfed their twins to get advice. There are MoMs groups in practically every city. Check out dadsguidetotwins.com/extras to find a group in your area.

If help is not available while establishing breastfeeding, Mom can always feed one baby at a time. Yes, it will be a little easier for her, but the tradeoff here is that she faces the reality of back-to-back feedings so she never gets a break.

Newborns, until they reach about two months old, need to eat every two to three hours. Your wife may very well feel like a milking machine that is running all day long as she feeds the babies one at a time.

Breastfeeding is a physical and emotional burden. Yes, it has wonderful benefits, but it is a burden nonetheless. So I reiterate: only do this if your wife wants to.

Even if you, as parents, decide to breastfeed the twins before the twins are born, be flexible and remember it is OK to change your mind.

My wife wanted to breastfeed, and even though it worked smoothly with each of our boys, it ended up not working so well with our twins. They had trouble latching on and getting a good suck due to short frenulums under their tongues. This made them frustrated and even more hungry. So we switched to bottle feeding the twins.

Bottle Feeding Option

If your wife wants to bottle feed the twins, or you have a change in plans, roll up your sleeves and prepare to get to work. You will become the master of making a bottle with one hand while holding a baby in the other.

Use nursing pillows or car seats to
help you feed both twins at once.

When we switched to bottle feeding, the first thing I noticed was that there was a lot of overhead in terms of preparing and cleaning. But it gave me a chance as a dad to hold and bond with each of my twin daughters while I fed them. (Yes, even in the middle of the night!)

With enough practice, you'll be able to hold and bottle feed both twins simultaneously. At that point, you can sit on the floor between your twins in their bouncy seats or car seats and hold a bottle in each of their mouths.

You Choose Together

Whatever choice you and your wife make together, be prepared to help and support your wife. If she carries the burden of breastfeeding, you need to be her assistant, helping her position babies, bringing burp clothes, making sure she has plenty to drink, etc., until everyone gets the hang of it.

If you choose to bottle feed, you'll both have your fair share of feedings both night and day.

Either way, take heart. The twins won't need help eating forever! Before they turn one, they will be feeding themselves.

FROM YOUR FELLOW FATHERS OF TWINS...
"My wife tried breastfeeding and then pumping and storing, but I guess supply couldn't keep up with demand. We had to go to bottle feeding relatively soon after we got home. Inside the first week we had to move to bottle feeding." - Dakota Hubbard

"Initially my wife was full steam ahead into breastfeeding. It worked out well for a couple of months while she was able to stay home on maternity leave. With two hungry boys it felt like we could never get ahead of the game. She had enough supply just to get through each feed each time and after she would try to pump. She would only get a few ounces each time. When we got close to her going back to work we made the decision that we would have to go to formula, just because we didn't have the supply and she didn't have the time at work to keep pumping.

It was really tough on us to make that decision. We know the research shows breastfeeding is the best, but there's still good outcomes either way. The twins tolerated the transition well. They moved on and developmentally they hit all their landmarks." - Steve Smith

Chapter Eight

Twin Dad Mindset

Get Ready for Sleep Deprivation

One of the most trying aspects of having newborn twins is sleep deprivation.

Sleep deprivation is torture.

Think about those old war or spy movies where the hero is literally tortured by being forced to stay awake. Just when the hero falls asleep, the bad guys wake him up.

You, my friend, are the hero. Unfortunately, your twins play the part of the torturer. Not that they don't love you. They just haven't learned to sleep through the night yet.

By the time we had our twins, we had already had two boys. Since they were both singletons, my wife ended up caring for them during the night because she was breastfeeding.

I didn't know how spoiled I was.

With twins, your wife can't do it all herself. This means that you will be working the night shift as well.

Since you will be up and down all night with your babies, you need to be ready to deal with sleep deprivation. It's time to make a plan.

Sleep When You Can

You must sleep when you get the chance. This means that when babies are asleep, you should be, too. You'll be tempted to get stuff done once the babies are asleep. That "stuff" can wait. Email is not as important as sleep. Your favorite TV show is not as important as sleep. Gaming is not as important as sleep.

You need a nap. Take it. Sometimes this means lying down at 7 p.m. Do it. Sacrificing some of your normal activities is a small price to pay for functionality.

Besides, your twins won't be the torturers forever – there will be a return to normalcy in your near future.

So sleep now.

Set Expectations

Sleep deprivation will lower your ability to work effectively, communicate properly, and live normally. This will impact the people around you. Set expectations with your coworkers, friends, and family.

Let everyone know that you aren't getting any sleep and that you won't be able to do X, attend Y, or deliver Z. Offer alternatives. Make compromises. But communicate the reason for your altered physical and mental state. Most people are very understanding.

Don't Take It Personally

Sleep deprivation will try your marriage like almost nothing else you've ever experienced. Since both you and your spouse will be tortured with no sleep, you must remember not to take anything personally.

If your wife snaps at you, it is because she is beyond tired. If something didn't get done like you liked it, blame the sleep deprivation.

You'll be a lot happier if you don't take anything personally while you and your spouse are under the effects of sleep deprivation. It will probably be the most charitable action you take in your marriage.

Your twin babies, while the source of your sleep deprivation, are not intentionally torturing you. So don't take your babies' actions personally either.

How Are You Doing?

After my paternity leave, I returned to work but was still suffering from sleep deprivation. Whenever anyone asked how I was doing, I answered, "I'm tired."

You'll be tired too. But hang in there. Your babies will start sleeping through the night, and you will, too.

FROM YOUR FELLOW PARENT OF TWINS...
"The sleep deprivation is UNREAL. It was the biggest surprise to me. It was by far the most difficult part of new motherhood. My husband and I devised a plan to take shifts. He would be responsible for all waking up/feedings up until 1-2am, and then my shift would start, and I would be responsible for all of the feedings."
- Mariam Barnes

Social Time Impact

Prepare yourself and your friends for a new social reality after the twins arrive.

You will disappear for the first several months with newborn twins as you try to keep your head above water and the family alive. For the first year, you'll be in a fog that will overtake your life.

Your wife and the twins will need your help, and that will mean inevitable sacrifices in your social life.

Avoid recurring commitments as your due date approaches. Stay flexible and set expectations with your friends. You'll disappoint fewer people, including yourself, if you are ready for a new social life post-twins.

Twins Are Harder than You Think

Your twins will be harder and more demanding than you think. And you know what? That is OK and completely normal.

It is nearly impossible to visualize the new life that will be ushered in with the birth of your twins. You'll do new things, experience problems, and conquer milestones that you never saw coming.

You will climb to a mountaintop and then do it again.

Take the days one at a time. Before you know it, the time will be flying and you'll be at a new stage of normalcy.

Clean House Expectations

Newsflash: Your house will be a mess with twins.

I remember when our house was always orderly and I could walk freely through the house without stepping on a hard plastic toy. Those days were B.C. (before children).

Before twins, your home may be a house of order and Zen-like peace. As a father of twins, now is the time to lower your expectations.

When your twins arrive, you will not be able to physically handle everything you once did. Some things will have to be let go or left undone.

A clean and orderly house can be let go.

You'll quickly realize that it is unrealistic to try to keep the house totally clean, especially during the day when the kids are awake.

My wife and I used to spend the hour after the kids went to bed (about 7 p.m.) doing tag-team cleaning every night. We started in the kitchen and cleaned up after dinner and then worked through the toy room and family room, picking up the random items the kids failed to put away. Then we went on to our evening routine.

We didn't necessarily love that we had to spend an hour every evening cleaning up, but we did appreciate the lower stress levels a clean kitchen gave to start of the next day.

We'd also rather spend time during the day playing and reading with the kids than cleaning. Granted, as the kids are getting older, we are involving them in more cleaning and chores. However, with newborn twins, you'll just have a mess.

Get used to the mess. Embrace it. Ignore it. Clear a pathway through it for those late night walks you'll take to care for a baby.

After a while, you'll be able to adjust to the new reality. Sometime after that your twins will be old enough to not only make a mess but clean it up too. Just lower your expectations between now and then, and you'll be fine.

How Twins Impact Your Laundry

Laundry time with twins means stacks of clothes.

Having twins means you will be doing more laundry. Just how much will depend on each twin, but I'm confident that your laundry will at least double. And no, not just double because there are two. It will likely double from what you are doing right now for the entire family.

We went from a family of four to a family of six when our twins were born and we doubled our laundry even though we only grew our family by 50 percent. We found ourselves running the laundry almost every day with newborn twins.

You will see several peaks in dirty laundry during your twins' early years. First, when they are newborns, they will often spit up on themselves (and you) or blow out their diapers. You will be changing their clothes, and possibly yours, multiple times per day, in addition to the burp cloths, blankets and bedding when these accidents occur.

Later on, you'll see another spike in laundry when the twins begin feeding themselves, and another when they begin potty training.

Today's Challenge is Only Temporary

At every stage of your twins' progress, from pregnancy onwards, there will be challenges. You'll deal with physical burdens, mental strain, marital frustrations, discipline issues, feeding problems, and tons of messes.

One way to keep your sanity is to remember that the current moment is only temporary.

There is an extra heavy dose of craziness with twins. Just remind yourself that it is only temporary and things will improve. Your twins will mature and become easier to care for. You will mature as a parent of twins and learn how to deal more easily with your twins.

I've noticed that things come in cycles with twins. You get a new challenge. It blows you away. After a short time you've adapted and it becomes normal for you. And just when things start to work smoothly, something else happens to break the routine and you repeat the cycle.

This is a natural evolution with twins. Each challenge is often just for a season. You won't have to feed your twins in the middle of the night forever. Likewise, when you potty train your twins, they will eventually master that skill — just like we all do.

Remember: right now is only temporary. You can deal with the challenge of now. You can handle the challenge that tomorrow brings ... tomorrow.

Enjoy each moment. Before you know it, your twins will be teenagers with a new set of challenges. Then you'll look back and think how easy it was to just change a pair of blow-out diapers or clean a spit-up mess.

Amazing Miracle

Even with all these difficulties, you will be fascinated by your twins. The miracle that brought them to your family will be very intriguing to you. You'll compare and contrast their different physical looks and personalities.

It is amazing that two little babies came at the same time. It is also amazing that they can be so different one moment and so similar the next.

Cherish the uniqueness of your twin situation. Not all dads get this opportunity.

I Can't Tell My Twins Apart

Don't feel bad if you can't tell your twins apart. This is especially challenging when you have identical twins. But if you've got fraternal twins, don't think you're off the hook. Swaddled newborns tend to look pretty similar even if they are different sexes.

It may very well take you weeks to be able to tell your twins apart effortlessly. And then, when you think you've mastered it, they will confuse you and you'll call out the wrong name again.

As your twins get older, you'll be able to tell them apart at a glance. But I've also been caught off guard when looking across the room and trying to distinguish between my girls, and I can't do it.

What I Didn't Expect With Twins

There have been some aspects of raising twins that are par for the course and pretty similar to our experience in raising our singletons. However, there have been some surprising things about twins, as well.

I have been surprised:

- By how big and uncomfortable my wife got during pregnancy
- By how many diapers we went through. It seems that they got used up as fast as we bought them.
- By how many people gawk at our family when we are all out in public
- That the girls do so many things the same and yet are so different

- By just how much we'd need that twin double stroller to control the chaos in public
- That I'd ever be able to tell my identical twin girls apart at a glance
- That my other kids were able to tell the twin girls apart before I could
- That sleep deprivation was worse than with a single-ton
- By how little time or energy I had to do anything but clean up the house after the kids are all in bed
- By the mountains of laundry that stack up
- By how much time it takes to get shoes on, jackets on, diaper bag packed, and everyone loaded into their car seats before we're ready to go somewhere
- At the amount of patience having two sick twins at the same time requires
- By how happy I am to be greeted by two smiling faces when I get home from work
- By how truly satisfying being a parent of twins is

A Journal as a Mental Outlet

Sometimes when you are burdened with the responsibilities of your twins and your mind is foggy, you may start to feel like you are going crazy.

There is an easy way for some self-therapy. You need to write. Don't worry, you don't need to start a blog and publish your thoughts publicly if you don't want to.

When I talk about writing, I mean a personal journal. From the moment you find out you are having twins, you should start writing.

Your entries don't have to be long. If you are used to updating your status on Facebook or sending a tweet on Twitter, writing a few lines in a journal shouldn't be too bad.

What can you write about? Anything that comes to mind. For example:

- things you are grateful for today
- ways someone else blessed your life today
- how you feel about your twins
- something funny your twins did
- how your other kids interact with your twins
- your goals for the future with your kids
- what you worry about
- what made you smile today
- a breakthrough you enjoyed today, at home or work

Think of your journal as your personal therapist. As you record little memories and thoughts from each day, you gain a better perspective of the good things that are actually happening. This will help pull you out of the daily fog you may find yourself in with twins.

As time goes on, you'll be able to look back at your journal and see details and remember things that you would have otherwise forgotten. Pictures and videos are great, but they don't always capture your thoughts, feelings, and memories like a journal can.

Start writing today. Just put down a sentence or a few words if that is all the time you have.

Your future you will thank you. And your twins will one day read their daddy's journal and thank you, too.

Taking Advice

You will find yourself swimming in a sea of information. Some will be self-imposed (Internet searching or asking advice from others) while other tidbits of information will be thrust upon you by well-meaning friends, family, and complete and total strangers.

We found a few things that helped us filter out unneeded, unwanted, or unnecessary information as we tried to make sense of our soon-to-be new reality.

1. If you hear the same advice from several people (three or more), listen up!

You will soon have your hands fuller than they have ever been. Don't reinvent the wheel. If you start to hear recurring themes in the advice you are receiving, they are worth listening to. Make notes and talk with your spouse about ways to implement the advice. You'll be glad you did.

2. When taking advice, try to find out how similar the situation is to your own.

This truly will help you filter out the inapplicable and help you set reasonable expectations for your experience.

A first-time parent of one baby has a huge learning curve. It takes a good, long while to figure everything out. A second-time parent tends to enjoy No. 2 a little more because they've "been there, done that" with the first. And so it goes, with each progressive addition getting a little easier to handle.

First-time parents that are expecting twins will be doubly overwhelmed. Parents of multiples falling a little farther down the birth order chain don't face the same challenges with the same intensity.

So if you take advice from someone whose twins were children 2 and 3, and yours are 1 and 2, be prepared for some disparity between their advice and your reality.

3. One person's experience is not necessarily generalizable to your own.

My wife talked to several women about breastfeeding twins prior to the birth of our twin girls. After our twins were born and we tried breastfeeding, my wife dealt with a lot of frustration because it wasn't working like everyone she talked to said it would. Upon reflection, this was due in large part to the fact that the women she talked with had twins as #1 and #2, or #2 and #3, not #3 and #4 like ours were. Having two other young children at home changed the reality and logistics of breastfeeding for us.

4. Make note of what works for you.

Others having twins after you will inevitably be asking for your advice!

You Are a Star with Twins

Get ready to be noticed with your twins. Everywhere you go, you'll be gawked at, pointed at, admired, and questioned by complete strangers.

You'll be particularly noticeable if you have your double stroller or have both twins in the same shopping cart at the store. Sure, the celebrities get all the headlines when they have twins, but you will be the star wherever you go.

As a father of twins, most people will ignore you if your wife is around and will direct all comments and questions to her.

So technically, your twins are the stars, and you are just their manager. Enjoy the attention while your twins are young because it fades over time.

People Ask Stupid Questions

There is something about walking around with twins that brings out the curious questions, stupid inquiries, and unsolicited comments from complete strangers. Be prepared for any and all of these questions and comments that will be randomly thrown at you when you are in public:

- Are they twins?
- Do twins run in your family?
- Are they identical?
- Were they planned?

- You've got your hands full!
- Were they born at the same time?
- What do you do when they are both crying?
- Which one was born first? Which one is older?
- Which one is this one?
- How do you tell them apart?
- Are these all yours?
- Are you done?
- Are they natural?
- Did you use fertility drugs?
- How did you get pregnant with twins?
- Which one is the good one?
- Did you know you were having twins?
- How do you do it?
- Do you have help?
- Do you like having twins?
- Is it hard having twins?
- References to Octomom or other TV series families with multiples. "They had 8 kids and you only have X, so it must be easy."

FROM YOUR FELLOW FATHER OF TWINS...
"The first one is: 'are they twins?' You know, that's always the first one. Sometimes I say 'yes' and move on and sometimes it's fun to mess with people a little bit and that's just how it goes. And there's the 'are they identical?' You know we don't have boy/girl twins, so we don't have to give people funny looks or anything.

Not that its anyone's business, but it's an easy question to answer so that one comes up quite a bit. Not a day goes by where you don't hear 'double trouble' and all of those same clichés that people like to throw out there. It just speaks to how novel twins are. I remember one day we went to the aquarium, we actually saw 3 other sets of twins. It was really funny because the kids were all looking at each other after seeing kids that were the exact same age and looking relatively the same. They were all eying each other up. It was even novel for them. I guess that it's human nature to be asking questions of strangers with twins in public." - Dave Macdonald

The Secret to Doing Anything with Twins

You'll probably hear incredulous comments from non-twin parents like, "How do you do it?" Well, as with anything in life, I find a way. That way contains the secret to doing anything with twins.

The secret? One at a time.

Need to change a poopy diaper on both twins? Change one at a time. Are both babies crying and you're home alone? Soothe one at a time. Spoon feeding both twins dinner? Take turns: one at a time.

Very rarely will you need to do whatever you are doing simultaneously with both twins. One exception would be if your house is on fire. Grab both twins and get out.

Need to load the twins into the car? One at a time. Need to teach them how to walk? Teaching them one at a time will make your life a lot easier. Time to potty train? One at a time.

Remember, twins may come two at a time but that doesn't mean they need to do everything at the same time. Just think, they weren't even born at the same exact time. How did they arrive? One at a time.

Conclusion

As a twin dad, you are part of an elite fraternity of men. The majority of dads never get to experience what you will with your twins.

There will be moments of joy, sadness, and complete exhaustion. But in the end, your little twins will be a magnificent blessing and you'll love them more than you thought you ever could.

Be ready to be an active participant in raising your twins. Your wife can't do it alone and she and your family need your help.

Your twins will push you to your physical limits in those early months. Don't ever be afraid to ask for help from others.

Focus on what really matters. Lots of activities, hobbies, entertainment, and chores can wait because they just aren't as important as taking care of your pregnant wife or newborn twins.

You will grow into your twin fatherhood and will master skills that other dads will find impossible.

Additional Resources for Twin Dads

As stated in the purpose of this book, other than what you're reading right now, there are very few resources for twin dads. However, here are some additional sources of information that I've found helpful.

Books

These books have made my life as a father—and a father of twins—infinitely easier than it would have been had I not read them:

- *The Sleep Lady's Good Night, Sleep Tight: Gentle Proven Solutions to Help Your Child Sleep Well and Wake Up Happy*, Kim West
- *Healthy Sleep Habits, Happy Twins*, Marc Weissbluth
- *Secrets of the Baby Whisperer: How to Calm, Connect, and Communicate with Your Baby*, Tracy Hogg
- *The Expectant Father: Facts, Tips and Advice for Dads-to-Be*, Armin Brott
- *Raising Twins: From Pregnancy to Preschool*, Shelly Vaziri Flais
- *Twins 101*, Khanh-Van Le-Bucklin

Don't feel like you have to read every book, cover to cover. Look at your learning as a "just-in-time learning." If the doctor tells you about a condition or concern, then go learn about it and dig into the details.

Online Forums

In addition to books, try searching online or posting on an online forum. Sometimes the best answers come from other parents that have been in your exact same shoes.

Babycenter.com has forums for parents of twins and even subgroups for those with due dates in certain months. You'll find mostly mothers here but even dads can extract some tips on how to keep Mom happy and insights into the twin pregnancy.

Social Media

Check out these great Facebook pages:

- Multiples and More
- Twiniversity
- Twin Pregnancy And Beyond

Facebook is also home to dozens of groups dedicated to fathers and parents of twins. Many of these groups are private so you can ask your questions without the entire world seeing.

If you enjoy listening to podcasts, Positive Parenting by author and parenting expert Armin Brott offers weekly insights and guidance on parenting: mrdad.com.

Local Groups

We, as fathers, can piggyback on organizations that mothers of multiples have to meet together with like-minded individuals. Look for a "Mothers of Twins", "Parents of Multiples" or similar group in your local area. Find a list via: dadsguidetotwins.com/extras

Even though the name says "Mothers of Twins," don't be scared away here, because these clubs often have subgroups within them where fathers can meet together for a dad's night out or get together as fathers for activities. These groups often welcome dads to their meetings or to their activities, so don't be too afraid to go and meet other dads of twins in your local area.

More From Dad's Guide to Twins

Listen to twin tips and discussions with fathers of twins on the Dad's Guide to Twins podcast: twindadpodcast.com

Connect via your favorite social media:

- twitter.com/twindadjoe

- facebook.com/dadsguidetotwins

- pinterest.com/twindadjoe

- instagram.com/twindadjoe

- youtube.com/dadsguidetotwins

Picture Credits

Unless otherwise noted, pictures by the author.

Author's picture with daughters by Rachel Campos.

Nayelli and Adrian Rodriguez provided pictures of the twin 3d ultrasound (p. 14), infant twins (p. 24), dad with twins (p. 38), baby bottles (p. 65), diaper stack (p. 69), inline stroller (p. 872), and laundry (p. 135).

Mandi and Bryce Winkelman provided pictures of the house (p. 58) and dad feeding twins (p. 125).

Twins in the NICU by Lori and James Burt (p. 115).

Read This Book Next...

The book you just finished helped you get through the twin pregnancy and prepare for your twins. Now the real adventure begins.

Pick up a copy of my next book, "Dad's Guide to Raising Twins: How to Thrive as a Father of Twins" which will walk you though the next several crazy, challenging and exciting years of raising twins.

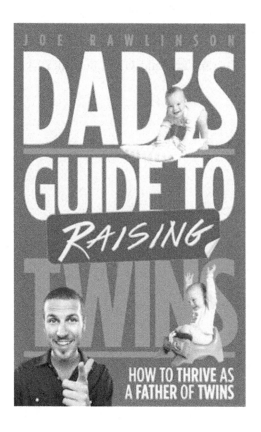

"Dad's Guide to Raising Twins" covers newborns, toddlers, through to potty training and more:

- **How to feed your twins and get them on a schedule** to keep them healthy and you sane. Tips on breast and bottle feeding your babies and introducing solid foods.

- **Encouraging individuality in your twins** and help them develop a solid sense of self. How to bond with your twins and appreciate their uniqueness.

- **How to travel with twins** at all stages of the early years. Tips for traveling on road trips and by plane and how to actually enjoy your trips!

- **Get your twins to sleep through the night.** What you need to do each night to overcome sleep troubles. How to create a great sleep routine for naps and night time.

- The **reality of diapering twins** with tricks to make that easier on you and your wallet. Plus learn how to graduate from diapers and potty train your twins.

- **Keep balance in your personal life** with twins while you juggle work and family life. It isn't easy but this book shows you how to do it.

Get your copy of "Dad's Guide to Raising Twins: How to Thrive as a Father of Twins" here:

dadsguidetotwins.com/raisingtwinsbook

Index

Get More Twin Tips Online

To thank you for reading my book, I want to share some more resources with you that are accessible online:

- **Free weekly newsletter** to help you be a better parent of twins

- **Week-by-week pregnancy guide** to eliminate surprises and help you know what to expect and prepare for

- **Specific twin gear recommendations** to help you get the best products for your twins and eliminate the stress of shopping

- **Dad's Guide to Twins podcast** so you can listen to tips and tricks wherever you are

- **Find a local parents of twins club** for extra support face-to-face with your fellow twin parents

To access these resources, visit:

dadsguidetotwins.com/extras

Made in the USA
Monee, IL
16 November 2021

82297771R00095